· · · ·

PRAISE FOR
Earth Magic

"A perfect gem of a book, encyclopedic in scope, and inspired in approach ... Covering the tangible magic of stone, plant, and tree along with the evocative magic of deity, mythological creatures, and sacred sites, *Earth Magic* provides an extensive range of tools, techniques, practices, and ideas that has potent potential to transform personal practice. This is a fabulous, hands-on, roll-up-your-sleeves, get-mucky, get-muddy celebration of Earth, and Dodie truly leaves no stone unturned ... With this book in one's hands, one cannot help but deepen, expand, and enliven one's personal Pagan practice."

—Tiffany Lazic, author of *The Great Work*

"Whether you are a beginner or a sage, this book widens, strengthens, and renews your connection to Mother Earth through multiple perspectives and practical applications from all around the globe and information dating back to the beginning of the human race. This educational book is a wonderful companion to any earth-based practice ... [It] brings awareness back to Mother Earth through the consciousness, application, and workings devoted to Gaia and the cycles in which she moves. This is a marvelous work of art!"

—Granddaughter Crow, author of
Wisdom of the Natural World

"Reading like a heartfelt love letter to Terra Mater herself, *Earth Magic* provides readers with a lush garden of information pertaining to the sacred element of earth. From wild plants and ancient stones to verdant spirits and terrestrial haunts, this book contains vital knowledge for anyone seeking to learn more about the enchantments of the natural world. With an abundance of helpful exercises and supportive tips along the way, Dodie Graham McKay masterfully instructs readers on practical ways to connect with nature, to dig deep into the dirt, to develop a well-rooted relationship with their landscape, and to wield the very magic of the element of earth itself."

—Kelden, author of *The Crooked Path*

"This excellent book will deepen and strengthen your relationship with the land you live on, the element of earth, and with planet Earth. Taking a deep dive into mythology, history, folklore, and symbolism of humanity's relationship with earth, the book invites you to explore your own relationship with this element."

—Yvonne Aburrow, author of *All Acts of Love and Pleasure: Inclusive Wicca; Dark Mirror: The Inner Work of Witchcraft;* and *The Night Journey: Witchcraft as Transformation*

"The book starts by wonderfully giving us permissions: to ponder our planet, our magic, and even to take notes directly in it. It begins on this firm foundation and only grows from there. McKay covers beings, places, myths and earth magic on every level. This is a must for any serious collection about magic and witchcraft."

—Lilith Dorsey, author *Water Magic* and *Orishas, Goddesses, and Voodoo Queens*

EARTH
MAGIC

© Toni Kotaska, Toni K Photography

Dodie Graham McKay (Treaty One Territory, Winnipeg, Canada) is an initiated Witch and independent filmmaker. Since the 1980s, she has been involved in magic, music, and other forms of media. Dodie is the founder of Moongazey Films Inc., has written for *The Wild Hunt*, and is active in her local art and magic communities.

EARTH MAGIC

DODIE GRAHAM McKAY

MAGIC

ELEMENTS
OF
WITCHCRAFT

Earth Magic © 2021 by Dodie Graham McKay. All rights reserved. No part of this book may be used or reproduced in any manner whatsoever, including internet usage, without written permission from Llewellyn Publications except in the case of brief quotations embodied in critical articles and reviews.

FIRST EDITION
Fourth Printing, 2024

Cover design by Shannon McKuhen
Interior illustrations by Llewellyn Art Department

Llewellyn is a registered trademark of Llewellyn Worldwide Ltd.

Library of Congress Cataloging-In-Publication Data

Names: McKay, Dodie Graham, author.
Title: Earth magic / Dodie Graham McKay
Description: First edition. | Woodbury, Minnesota : Llewellyn Publications,
  a division of Llewellyn Worldwide, Ltd., [2021] | Series: Elements of
  witchcraft | Includes bibliographical references and index. | Summary:
  "This book concerns itself solely with the element of earth. Like The
  Witch's Flame, this book will focus on the history of the element in
  magic, religion, and spiritual work, its place in folklore, modern
  practice, and pop culture. Manifestations of the element include: rocks,
  crystals, dirt, the pentacle, the body, trees and herbs and the Earth
  itself - depending on tradition"-- Provided by publisher.
Identifiers: LCCN 2021028403 (print) | LCCN 2021028404 (ebook) | ISBN
  9780738764320 (paperback) | ISBN 9780738764559 (ebook)
Subjects: LCSH: Magic. | Witchcraft. | Nature--Miscellanea.
Classification: LCC BF1623.N35 M35 2021 (print) | LCC BF1623.N35 (ebook)
  | DDC 133.4/3--dc23
LC record available at https://lccn.loc.gov/2021028403
LC ebook record available at https://lccn.loc.gov/2021028404

Llewellyn Worldwide Ltd. does not participate in, endorse, or have any authority or responsibility concerning private business transactions between our authors and the public.

All mail addressed to the author is forwarded but the publisher cannot, unless specifically instructed by the author, give out an address or phone number.

Any internet references contained in this work are current at publication time, but the publisher cannot guarantee that a specific location will continue to be maintained. Please refer to the publisher's website for links to authors' websites and other sources.

Llewellyn Publications
A Division of Llewellyn Worldwide Ltd.
2143 Wooddale Drive
Woodbury, MN 55125-2989

www.llewellyn.com
Printed in the United States of America

Dedicated to the members of
Boreal Heart Coven—past, present, and future—
for the magic, the friendship,
and the love of the Craft

and

to Jeff, with all my love,
for supporting the
noisy bunch of witches
in the basement.

CONTENTS

PART 3:
RECIPES, RITUALS & SPELLCRAFT

DISCLAIMER

The author and publisher are not responsible for the use or misuse of the plants and botanicals listed in this book, especially those labeled as TOXIC or POISONOUS. Even touching some of these plants can cause a negative reaction. The botanicals and plants listed here are included with their warnings in order to give a comprehensive study of these items.

All plants and botanicals, just like traditional medicines, may be dangerous when used improperly and or excessively over time. Be sure to understand completely what you are working with, use only fresh herbs from a trusted and sustainable source, and be aware that strengths may vary.

The author and the publisher do not endorse or guarantee the curative effects of any of the subjects presented in this work.

FOREWORD

For centuries and through many esoteric practices, the elements have been the cornerstones of magical practice. Whether it's ancient astrology or modern Witchcraft, these four basic elements create the boundaries and structures for larger, multidimensional spiritual frameworks.

Earth is the ground we walk on, quite literally. It is the rocks, the mud, and the mountains. Earth is also our body and our physical manifestation in this life. Earth is our centre, our money, and our stability.

Fire is the flame in the hearth. It is the candle, the bonfire, the sun. Fire both warms and destroys. It has the power to transform and incite. Fire is the flame of passion and our will to go on.

Water is the rain from the skies. It is the world's oceans, lakes, and rivers. It is a comforting bath, and the morning dew. Water is our blood, sweat, and tears. It rules our emotions and manifests as memories.

Air is all around us. It is the sounds we hear and the wind that touches our faces. Air carries seeds and pollen and the scents that both warn and delight. Air is our voice, our thoughts, and our ideas.

While every esoteric system applies these basic concepts differently, the elements are there, helping to structure practice and develop a greater understanding of self. For modern witches, the elements are often represented in their magical tools, where, for example, the cauldron might be water and the pentacle earth. For Wiccans more specifically, the elements help raise the magical circle and empower the protective quarters. In tarot, the elements flow through the symbolic imagery in the cards; and in astrology, the elements correspond to the signs. For still others, the elements simply provide spiritual guidance for daily meditations, visualizations, spell work, or life lessons. What element might you need to get through today, one might ask.

The following book is the fourth in a series that will dive deeply into the symbolism and spiritual usc of the elements from time long ago to today. Each book will focus on just one element, beginning with water. The books cover everything associated with the element from spiritual places and deities to practical spells and rituals. For the witch who wants to dive deeper into elemental practice or for someone who needs a first resource, this first book and its sisters will provide everything you need.

Written by four different authors from around the globe, the four books in the elemental magic series will show you just how wide and deep the esoteric understanding of the elements go and how to make their fundamental lessons work for your own magical and spiritual needs.

Join us on a deep exploration and journey of the magical use of the four elements.

By Heather Greene
ACQUISITIONS EDITOR, LLEWELLYN WORLDWIDE

INTRODUCTION

On December 24, 1968, the astronauts of the Apollo 8 space mission were celebrating Christmas Eve by orbiting the Moon. As their spacecraft emerged from the dark side of the Moon, our home, planet Earth, appeared over the Moon's horizon. Astronaut Bill Anders took up his camera and captured a defining photograph. The image depicts the grey and cratered surface of the Moon in the foreground, while floating in the inky black background, alone in the depths of space, sits a small and exquisitely beautiful blue and white planet.

The colour image was one of a kind. These were the days before satellite images took away the need for a human photographer to get lucky and be in the right place at the right time. There was no digital copy to distribute in seconds. His film needed to be returned to Earth and developed. New Year's 1969 was celebrated before the world got to share what had already changed the astronauts' lives.

Planet Earth. Our biosphere appears as a faint blue halo, like a planetary aura. Swirling white clouds, vast blue oceans, and a blush of sandy brown highlighting Africa. A sharp line reveals more than half of the planet is experiencing daylight while the rest of the globe is shrouded in the dark of night. All our history, present, and future are captured, every creature, plant, rock, and drop of water. All of humanity, save for the three sitting in the spacecraft, together in one extraordinary picture.

The photograph was dubbed "Earthrise" and it went on to become known as one of the most important pictures ever taken. It was humanity's first chance to see our planet in context and gain some perspective on the delicate beauty of where we live. The photo went on to become iconic, and was seen around the world on television, magazine covers, school textbooks, encyclopedias, and newspaper articles everywhere. But Bill Anders gave us more than just an awe-inspiring photograph that day; he gave the average person an opportunity to glimpse something much more, something that only the elite few who have travelled to space have experienced: the Overview Effect.

Space philosopher and author Frank White coined the term "Overview Effect" in 1987 to describe the phenomenon experienced by astronauts when they see Earth from space.[1] These space travellers that White interviewed consistently reported that after leaving the earth and having the ability to see it in its entirety from far up above, they experienced a shift in consciousness. The emotional response to seeing all of humanity drifting in space, with all the vast emptiness around it, is said to be one of tremendous connection and awe.

Seen from space, our planet has no borders, no divisions, and no walls. It is one planet, one home, unified and beautiful, shrouded in a shockingly thin protective layer of atmosphere that gives its flora and fauna the gift of life. How could this not have a life-changing impact on those few souls fortunate enough to blast off in a rocket ship to witness it? Why does a human being need to go to such an extreme to have this profound shift in consciousness?

1   Frank White, *The Overview Effect: Space Explorations and Human Evolution* (Boston: Houghton Mifflin, 1987).

We have all had moments when the day-to-day grind of our regular life calls for us to take a step back and regroup. This shift in perspective may be something as simple as walking away from an argument, taking a vacation, or turning our phone off. On some level we all understand that, in order to take stock of the things that really matter to us, we need to see the big picture. For the astronauts who get the gift of experiencing the Overview Effect firsthand, they are having the most epic "time out" a human being can imagine.

What can this teach us, as witches, Pagans, magical practitioners, or tree-hugging earth lovers? I think it is a wake-up call. The lessons we can learn from being aware of the big picture for our planet and choosing mindfully to consider it are keys to empowering our spiritual practices and the whole of our lives. When we honour and accept the interconnectedness of humanity with the natural world, and our place within the universe, we get our own overview of the potential available to us. We can embrace the enormity of it and work our magic to find ways to connect to the energies inherent around us and empower the magic we do to manifest the world we want to live in.

A few years ago, I made a documentary film, *Starry Nights*, about amateur astronomers. During the making of the project, I was able to travel to several small observatories in British Columbia to meet with the astronomy enthusiasts who manage these places and learn about their passion for the stars. I had some preconceived notions about the types of things we would talk about—telescopes, planets, stars—astronomy stuff. We did discuss those things, but more often than that we talked about Earth. The kind and welcoming people I met all had a story or two about how, when they realized how small our planet is in the context of space, they felt humbled and awestruck. Everyone had a moment when they looked through the telescope and realized how completely amazing it is. That somehow, our planet underwent exactly the right set of circumstances to create and sustain life. This may not be the same Overview Effect that the astronauts experience on space flights, but speaking to these astronomers, and then having my own opportunity to look through the big telescopes and see the depths of space with my own eyes, I was certainly overcome with emotion and an acute sense that the ground I was standing on was more alive, more vital, and more sacred than it had ever been to me before.

In this book, we will look at the ways to expand our perspective of what "Earth" means to us and how to apply this to the practice of magic. What defines earth as an element? What does stewardship of our Mother Earth have to do with our magical practices? How can we plug into the inherent energies of the earth and use it to empower our magic and improve our lives? This book will provide reference information for different symbols and manifestations of the earth element that you can work into your own practice.

Journal Your Connection with Earth

As you read through these chapters, I encourage you to take notes. Write down your observations in a journal and revisit them later. Give yourself permission to change your mind and revise your notes. We see in nature that nothing is born fully formed. Growth happens! Let your journal be a document to your own earthy growth.

Earth manifests in tactile and sensual pleasures, so find a journal that appeals to you, with nice paper to write on. Decorate and personalize your journal, making it as visually appealing as you want to. Find a pen to write with that is comfortable to hold and enjoyable to shape your words with. Experiment with fountain pens, inject some colour with pencil crayons, draw pictures and get creative. Make a journal that you will be excited to use.

Your copy of this book you are reading is also an opportunity to make notes. If you are like me, you probably take pretty good care of the books you acquire. Occasionally I give myself permission to use a book as a working tool and have fun with it. So, I am passing this permission on to you. Write in the margins of the pages of this book, use a highlighter, and underline things. Be messy and creative as you customize your copy and let it stand alongside your journal as a souvenir of your growing relationship with the element of earth.

I would suggest that this is the first lesson of earth: create a historical record. Just as the planet is built on layers and layers of rock and sediment, creating a geological story of its growth, you can write down and record your journey through what you read. Make notes about the information and practical work outlined in these pages. When you are done with this work, go back and review what you have written and mine it for nuggets of inspiration and insight.

Modern Witchcraft and Pagan traditions are often referred to as "Earth-based" paths. This implies that at the centre of the religious, spiritual, and/or magical practice there is a focus on Earth itself. This can take on many forms, from planning your celebrations around natural events and cycles to honouring Earth as a divine being. This divinity is often seen as female, the all-encompassing Earth Mother figure. It is this connection to the actual, tangible, and visible earth around us that draws many people to learn about and practice these traditions.

What do you associate with the word "earth"? Our planet? Dirt? Do you see images of gnomes in your mind's eye, or round and fertile mother goddess figures? Do you envision green and verdant gardens bursting with fruits and vegetables, or rocky mountain clefts? Do you see earth as a cold and dry element as the ancient Greeks did? Or do you envision it as a single complex living and breathing entity known as Gaia?

Finding your place with Earth—as an element, as your home, or as the embodiment of the Divine—begins with understanding your place in it and building on that relationship. The practice of just about any Witchcraft or Pagan path will benefit from taking the time to attune yourself to the natural earth energies around you and creating sympathy and connection with the forces at work in your environment. This is not as daunting as it may sound. Start by thinking about the place where you live.

Imagine that you have company coming from out of town, and your guest is also a witch with as deep an interest as you in connecting to the land they are presently occupying. Imagine how the conversation would go if they started asking these questions:

1. Describe the geology of this area. Think about the ground beneath your feet. Is it loose sandy soil, or hard packed clay? Is your area on a flood plain, or the side of a granite mountain?

2. What are the notable geographical features? Do you have mountains, rivers, or forests that define your area? What are their names?

3. Who were the first people of your area? What Indigenous groups populated your region before modern settlement occurred? Do you represent the Indigenous or settler population?

4. What are the local ancient sacred sites? Are there standing stones, sacred wells, petroforms, or mounds nearby?

Are these naturally occurring places, or built by humans? Who built them and why?

5. What is the local lore about land spirits or supernatural creatures? All around the world there are stories of other beings that inhabit the landscape and influence the people, animals, and land.

6. Name three native trees/flowers/plant medicines. This can be a bit tricky as we often have plants and trees growing around us that have been imported to our areas and have settled in so well that they feel like they have always been there.

7. Name three native animals/birds/fish. Even in large cities, animals find a way to make their homes.

8. At approximately what calendar date does each season actually seem to set in? This won't necessarily be in synch with the solstices or equinoxes. Try to pinpoint when it *feels* like the change of season has occurred.

The purpose of this exercise is to check in with yourself and see just how aware you are of where your most basic resources come from and whether you understand how the features of your local landscape fit together. We use these resources and our landscapes not only in our daily mundane life, but in our magical practices as well. It is a really good idea to know what they are and where they come from.

Write down this list of questions in your journal. Try answering as many as you can without doing any research. Once you have written down your answers to the best of your current knowledge, take a second look at the questions. This time around, use whatever research tools you are most comfortable with to fill in any blanks you may have left and to correct any errors. As your knowledge grows over time, review your progress, and make notes about new information as you receive it. Try going through this list of questions if you travel to new places.

The intention of this book is to present some information and techniques that can enrich your connection to the earth element. As you read, I do encourage you to try the exercises, ritual work, and suggestions that come up. Making things, cooking things, brewing things, grounding and centring, evoking the deities, maintaining a journal, and mindfully practicing magic are the sensual, tactile experiences that create effective changes in our environments and within ourselves. Doing these things with an eye turned toward observing the patterns and seasonal changes around us and how they relate to each other will help you build your own overview of how the magic of earth influences our lives.

PART
1
@

HISTORY,
FOLKLORE & MYTH

Chapter 1

EARTH THROUGHOUT TIME AND CULTURE

In this chapter we will take a look at some of the different manifestations of the element of earth and how they have influenced the magical and spiritual practices of human beings. On the most basic level, Earth is our planet, our home. We have always shaped and manipulated the land around us and built things to make ourselves more comfortable and as tributes to the things we worship and value. On a symbolic level, earth represents being stable, grounded, and close to nature. It relates to materialism and the physical manifestation of our thoughts, actions, and desires.

Creation

Since the beginning of our time on earth, human beings have tried to explain and understand how our planet came into being. We have told stories and created myths in an attempt to understand, document, and control our world, other people, and the creatures in it. Creation myths are the basic foundation for how a culture views the world. They create a common language, symbols, and identity for the group of people that they represent. There have been countless cultures on the earth since this storytelling began, spread around the world, and separated by time and distance. Despite this, the myths of how planet Earth was created by these cultures bear some similar themes that document some remarkable similarities.

Professor Marta Weigle, an anthropologist and folklorist, detailed in her book *Creation and Procreation: Feminist Reflections on Mythologies of Cosmogony and Parturition*, that there are nine different types of creation myths:

1. Accretion or conjunction—in which the classical elements somehow combine to create

2. Secretion—the bodily fluids of a divine being manifest a creation

3. Sacrifice—a sacrifice made by a deity triggers creation

4. Division or consummation—myths that feature sexual union, the hatching of an egg, or the division of parts of the universe

5. Earth-diver—a deity or creature dives into water to retrieve some matter that is used to establish or re-establish the earth

6. Emergence—the first inhabitants of the earth emerge from another place to create our world

7. Two creators—the world is made by two deities either in cooperation or competition

8. *Deus faber*—"God the Maker." The world is crafted by a deity, like a work of art

9. *Ex nihilo*—"from or out of nothing." Deity creates the world through their words or will[2]

2   Marta Weigle, *Creation and Procreation: Feminist Reflections of Mythologies of Cosmogony and Parturition* (Philadelphia: University of Pennsylvania Press, 1989).

In these myths, the creation of our world is described in one of, or a combination of, these nine concepts. One of the most widespread concepts is the earth-diver as the creator. This theme echoes across Eastern Europe, Siberia, northeast India, and North America. Across these varied cultures we hear stories of an assortment of creatures diving down into the vast oceans of a landless earth to bring up some matter from the bottom and create an environment for humans and animals to live on.

The Haudenosaunee (Iroquois) story of Sky Woman is an example of such a tale. Many variations of this myth exist but they all have the same earthy themes, in which we see Sky Woman as a creator, a mother, and a goddess figure.

Sky Woman

Long ago the world was covered by nothing but water and inhabited by water creatures and birds that could fly above it. High above the water there lived the Sky People. One day, after discovering she was pregnant with twins, Sky Woman stumbled and fell through a hole, grabbing seeds and roots as she went, and began to fall toward the waters. Down below, the water animals and birds could see the light from the hole high above and the falling figure of Sky Woman. The animals rallied together to see if they could help her and sent birds up to guide her down; they called on Turtle to give her a safe place to land. When Sky Woman landed, she was so grateful for their help, but she needed land in order to survive. And so, one by one, the animals tried to get her some by diving down deep into the water in search of some mud from the bottom. Eventually one of the animals—some say it was Muskrat, some say it was Otter, and others think it was Toad—managed to bring up a mouthful of mud. Sky Woman placed it on the back of Turtle and began to sing and dance. She planted the seeds and roots she had grabbed when she fell. As she sang and danced the mud increased and spread, creating the land we now call Turtle Island (or as some call it, North America). When the twins were born, they fought and competed. As they did this, all of creation was made, leaving the earth in balance. Then humans were made to be caretakers of this earth and maintain the balance and take good care of Mother Earth.

Prehistory

The earth itself became a place of shelter and community for our distant ancestors, who used caves as dwelling places. Evidence of human habitation in caves has been found all around the world, from Australia to Europe, Africa, and North America.

The human presence in caves is documented by the artifacts and artwork that they left behind. At the Altamira Caves in Spain, images of horses and bison were etched in ochre and charcoal along with handprints of the artists who made them more than 35,600 years ago. At Laas Gaal in Somalia, images of cows that appear to be wearing ceremonial garments, a giraffe, and domesticated dogs accompany human figures in paintings that are estimated to be between eleven thousand and five thousand years old. The Rock Shelters of Bhimbetka in India contain a trove of paintings dating back as far as twelve thousand years ago and as recent as the medieval period. The pictures show animals such as tiger, bison, monkeys, elephants, and antelopes as well as scenes of dancing, hunting, and collecting honey.

The most famous of the painted caves is located near the village of Montignac in the southwest of France. The Lascaux Cave complex features paintings of deer, aurochs, bison, horses, and ibex, and was decorated during the Palaeolithic period, around 17,000 to 15,000 BCE. More than six hundred images adorn the walls, including an image of a bull that is 5.2 meters (17 feet) long, making it the largest animal painting ever found in a cave.

The degree of artistic sophistication and the skill it would have taken to complete these paintings indicate that the reasons for going to such trouble and taking such care must have been of profound importance to the artists and the communities that they represented. Working in a dark cave with only some form of firelight could not have been easy. Some of the images in many of the painted caves that have been discovered are high overhead, or in awkward and hard to reach locations. We can only guess at why these paintings were made. Theories suggest that they may have ritual or religious significance or were some form of sympathetic magic to ensure a successful hunt. Whatever the motivation, the appearance of such artwork in so many diverse locations of the world says something about an inherent human desire to retreat to the shelter of the cave and leave a document of their connection to the land and the animals behind.

Ancient Greek philosophers believed that everything in the world was composed of what we now refer to as the four classical elements: earth, air, fire, and water. Eventually they added a fifth element: aether, or spirit. The symbolism and correspondences that came from this system have carried through time and are still referred to today by magical practitioners and scientists alike.

During the medieval period, Christianity was replacing paganism in large parts of the world. As the saying goes, "history is written by the victors," so much of what we understand about the pre-Christian practices, cults, and religions of the people was documented through a Christian filter; it was also largely written by men, from a particularly male perspective. Books were reserved for the elite few who had the money and privilege to acquire education and learn to read and write. The institutions of learning were just not available to women or the common folk who still carried the folk traditions and practices of the time. Much of the earthy lore of these practices and beliefs survived as oral history, or has been reconstructed by archeologists and academics, working with the physical remains of the time, combined with the oral lore that has been passed down.

The practice of alchemy was alive and well during this period, and members of the educated elite were blending their knowledge of science and philosophy with mysticism. Alchemists were experimenting with the idea that everything on earth was made of a certain combination of the four classical elements and if you could find a way to combine them properly, you could create anything. The secrecy and mystery surrounding alchemists attracted occult-minded people as well as the suspicion of the Catholic Church. The legacy of this for modern witches and Pagans is a system of magical correspondences attributed to the elements that is still recognized and used today by practitioners of many traditions.

By the late seventeenth century, medieval superstition had faded away into a new type of thinking that began to challenge the status quo and question the oppressive authority of the time. These new ways of thinking during the Age of Enlightenment created social change on a grand scale and ultimately led to the revolutions in France and America. This was also a time when secret societies like the Freemasons, the Illuminati, and the Rosicrucians began to gain popularity within European and North American society. These organizations blended secrecy, occult wisdom, ceremonial structure, and new ways of thinking, along with networking opportunities and fellowship. These concepts and structures informed the early Pagan revival as many of the founders of the early Witchcraft and Pagan movements were either members of or inspired by these organizations. These organizations also were responsible for constructing buildings to meet in and for publishing books for their members. While not necessarily wide in circulation, it was a hint of what was to come for occult readers in the future.

As Witchcraft and Paganism entered modern times, the world was a rapidly changing place. Advances in technology and culture were moving at an increasing speed, and the planet was about to be drastically affected by two world wars. Nature and a return to the rustic and earth was being romanticized in art, poetry, and literature. This growing nostalgia for a connection to the visible and invisible natural world was building as humanity entered the twentieth century.

In Western societies, this era saw a surge in interest for all things metaphysical and occult. Many people, unsettled by the events in the world around them, sought answers from mediums, psychics, and spirits. The popularity and increasing acceptance for methods such as tarot card readings, seances, tea-leaf readings, palm readings, and astrology were an indication that people wanted answers and guidance beyond what the established institutions of their societies could provide for them. Change was happening, and things that had previously only been discussed in hushed whispers as superstition, nonsense, or worse were now gaining ground as a viable alternative.

Throughout these same Western societies there have always been traditions of magic that have been present in one form or another. Every culture has some kind of tradition of folk medicine, charms, curses, or some kind of wise folk who are capable of healing people or animals as well as either causing or removing trouble by some supernatural means. These folks possess a knowledge of how to manipulate the natural world in some way to achieve their goals, or the goals of someone who would employ them to do so.

This work was usually performed privately, and intimate knowledge of the lore and traditions were kept to selected individuals. By the middle of the twentieth century, this was also going to change in a way that nobody could have predicted at the time.

Our ancestors may have built great temples to the gods, or stone circles and statues depicting various deities, but in the twentieth century a different version of Pagan and Witchcraft culture emerged. A large body of shared knowledge and a new tradition of open-source learning from widely published books and periodicals burst into the public eye. Organizations began to form and campaign for the same rights as mainstream religions. Pagans began to build infrastructure, dedicated libraries, resource centres, and even educational institutions where Pagans could learn how to become recognized clergy. Some went to so far as to purchase land and create Pagan retreats or campgrounds. When this started to happen, it blossomed very quickly. The demand for these resources and places was becoming quite clear.

In 1951 the Witchcraft Act was repealed in Britain, and it was no longer illegal to be a witch and practice witchcraft. This was the freedom that a retired, middle-aged man named Gerald Gardner needed in order to publish a book on the subject and proclaim himself publicly to be a witch.

While Gardner was by no means the only witch actively practicing his craft at that time, he was the loudest. He became a spokesperson, actively promoting witchcraft to the media. This attention worked like a beacon, attracting other interested people from all over the world to the modern Witchcraft movement. From this point forward, the modern movement gained momentum and the building of modern Pagan and Witchcraft institutions began in earnest. Things began to manifest, and a Neopagan culture was born that began to demand resources, infrastructure, and education.

While this list of institutions and organizations is by no means complete, it does represent the new world of Pagan- and Witchcraft-related resources that are being established. These things represent earth: they are the foundation of our communities, the fertility of our creativity and imagination, and they represent the abundance and nourishment that sustains our traditions and practices. The Neopagan movement blossomed and grew very quickly, which speaks to the strength of the desire of the people involved to establish and build true systems and culture.

Churches and Organizations

As Pagans' and Wiccans' efforts toward acceptance by mainstream society increased, so did the demand for formal education and training. Most Wiccan traditions, for example, have a closed system for training their priesthood. A trained high priestess or high priest can initiate and train a new Wiccan, but this authority and education is exclusive to that coven and has no official standing in the outside world. As Witchcraft and Paganism spread and gained popularity throughout the 1970s, particularly in North America, people started looking for the type of official training that other religions offered. Organizations with national and international profile also began to emerge for the purpose of helping seekers find teachers and groups to work with, and to advocate for Witchcraft and Pagan traditions and practitioners.

One of the oldest Pagan churches to be founded in the United States was the Church of All Worlds (CAW), incorporated in 1968. The church's founder, Oberon Zell, also promoted the creation of a new Pagan culture through *Green Egg Magazine* and Mythic Images, a Pagan statuary company. Other churches were soon to follow. The Covenant of the Goddess was formed in the United States in 1975 to serve as a national body dedicated to ensuring that witches and Wiccans have access to the rights and privileges that mainstream religions do. This network includes local councils throughout the US, Canada, the UK, and Australia that provide ritual and educational offerings.

The Wiccan Church of Canada (WCC), located in Toronto, Ontario, was legally recognized as a church in Canada in 1979. In 1980, high priestess Tamarra James became the first Wiccan priestess to be allowed to provide religious visitation in a Canadian jail. Along with her husband Richard, they also opened the Occult Shop and founded the Odyssean Tradition, which has consistently offered training and public classes for the past forty years. The WCC is now credited as being Canada's oldest and largest Wiccan organization.

Another influential American Pagan church is the Aquarian Tabernacle Church (ATC), which was also founded in 1979 and is not only a tradition unto itself, but also serves as an umbrella group, providing resources and legal support to other Wiccan and Pagan groups. The ATC is recognized legally as a church in the US and in Canada, South Africa, Australia, and Ireland. The ATC also sponsors the Woolston-Steen Theological Seminary, which offers ministerial education, and the Spiral Scouts, an organization for children like the mainstream Scouts organization, but with a Pagan worldview.

Not all Pagan organizations are churches. The Pagan Federation was founded in the United Kingdom in 1971 to advocate on behalf of the Pagan community and fight the negative stereotypes that were rife at the time, and that unfortunately still linger today. The Pagan Federation International (PFI) was created later, as an international umbrella organization with membership in at least twenty-three countries and representing a wide variety of Pagan traditions. In addition to fulfilling the same role as the Pagan Federation, the PFI acts as a resource for connecting interested seekers and active practitioners worldwide.

The Doreen Valiente Foundation speaks to the emerging importance of documenting and preserving our recent Pagan history before the memories of them slip away. Doreen is credited with being "The Mother of Modern Witchcraft." Her books and poems have shaped the way Wicca, and by extension, modern Witchcraft, and many forms of Paganism, are practiced. When she died in 1999, she bequeathed her collection of magic- and Wicca-related items to John Belham-Payne, the high priest she was working with up until her death. John and his wife Julie were the founders of the Centre for Pagan Studies, an organization dedicated to providing educational lectures on magic and folklore. The items were committed to a charitable trust they created, The Doreen Valiente Foundation, with the intention to make sure these items could be viewed and appreciated by the public without the threat of being lost, exploited, or sold off.

The growth of organizations led to a need for people to have places to gather. Occult shops became resource centres, their spaces becoming a haven for seekers to find an opportunity to find community, teachers, and like-minded folk. Just about every community of any size in the Western world has some kind of business offering wares that appeal to the magically inclined. Tarot cards, candles, herbs, and books catering to the Pagan and Witchcraft buyer are also finding their way into mainstream big-box bookstores, a clear indication that the appetite for these material goods is in demand and profitable. But the community's demand for Pagan-friendly spaces quickly outgrew the confined spaces inside shops, and the desire to gather outdoors, in close communion with nature and the earth, led to the establishment of outdoor facilities owned and operated by Pagans. The quest for Pagan-owned land to provide Pagan cultural and spiritual activities was on.

Pagan Land for Pagan Folk

Many Pagan folks like to get outdoors and participate in festivals. Throughout the summer season, events ranging from one day to a week or more take place usually on land that has been rented for the occasion and can include camping as part of the package. The desire to create permanent Pagan-friendly environments has compelled a few individuals and groups to invest in the land to make this a reality. The Circle Sanctuary Nature Preserve was founded in 1974 and it encompasses many of the resources that the rapidly growing Pagan community was looking for. Located on two hundred acres of countryside in southwestern Wisconsin, USA, the land provides a place for an annual festival, classes, and seasonal rituals. One of the first "green cemeteries" in the US is also located at Circle Sanctuary, providing witches, Pagans, and others who revere nature with a sympathetic place to be buried and memorialized. Covering twenty acres, the cemetery also provides a special area for fallen military Pagans. The grave markers for these are supplied by the US Department of Veterans Affairs and, thanks to the efforts of the Lady Liberty League, an advocacy group led by Reverend Selena Fox, the founder of Circle Sanctuary, military grave markers can now include either a pentacle for witches, Wiccans, and Pagans, or an awen, for Druids.

Located in southern Ontario, Canada, on one hundred acres of land along the Bonnechere River sits Raven's Knoll, a Pagan-owned and -operated campground and event centre. It was founded in 2009 to provide a venue for Canada's largest Pagan festival, Kaleidoscope Gathering, and it also hosts smaller festivals and events virtually every weekend from May until September. The owners of this land, Austin Lawrence and Marianne Pearce, have created a unique atmosphere that is not specific to any one Pagan tradition, with a strong emphasis on community building and participation. The land features sacred sites and shrines representing many different traditions, and everything is maintained with the support of volunteers. Large ventures like Circle Sanctuary and Raven's Knoll are rare, but as the Pagan movement grows, the infrastructure and culture that forms around it will grow as well.

Fighting for Nature

Modern Paganism has some strong connections with the environmental movement. As we moved through the twentieth century and the damage being caused by humans was rapidly becoming impossible to ignore, the line between nature-worshipping Pagans and environmental activists began to fade. The people who worshipped Earth as our mother began to fight for her. Scientist and writer James Lovelock published the book *Gaia: A New Look at Life on Earth* in 1979 and it detailed what is now referred to as "Gaia Theory." His work on this began in the 1960s and it presents a theory that suggests that the earth could be considered as a single living organism, and that all life and systems on it play a part in maintaining and regulating the conditions that comfortably sustain life. His 1975 article presenting his theory, which was published in the *New Scientist*, gave his theory some traction, and the attention of other scientists and critics alike. His published version of Gaia Theory was predated by another vision of our Earth Mother, Gaea, that came to Oberon Zell. In 1971 he published his own paper, entitled "TheaGenesis" in his magazine *The Green Egg*, in which he also described that all life on Earth was one living and sentient being. Both theories provide insight and inspiration on both scientific and spiritual levels and reference for Pagan earth activists.

A guiding voice in the earth-based spirituality movement is Starhawk, whose books and actions have taught Neopagans and activists the fundamentals of magic, activism, and goddess worship. Her collaboration with permaculture designer Penny Livingston-Stark has evolved into Earth Activist Training, a program that teaches effective skills to organize people and heal the planet through permaculture. This is a system that is based on designing and implementing systems that are in sympathy with the patterns of nature for the benefit of people and the environment. It emphasizes sustainable ways to secure food, shelter, resources, and community.

Where you find efforts to preserve the planet and heal the harm done by industry and civilization, you will find Pagans. A global movement known as The Warrior's Call was instigated by Pagans in the UK to protest fracking and extreme drilling techniques. In 2015, a group of Pagans published the Pagan Community Statement on the Environment, which was signed and supported by thousands of Pagan folks internationally, being translated into sixteen languages and endorsed by many leaders within the community. As difficult as it can be to get the diverse personalities and traditions within the Pagan movement to agree unanimously on one thing, care and concern for Earth may be the one exception. The practice of environmentalism enables modern Pagans to elevate their stated reverence for Earth into action in the real world.

• • • •

Beginning

Not every Pagan or witch is an environmental activist, and few of us are born that way. There is usually some crossroads that we find ourselves at, where we decide to change, and take up the fight to preserve and protect our Mother Earth.

Sparrow Kemp is a Wiccan high priestess, healer, activist, and co-host of the Wigglian Way podcast. She lives in the beautiful and environmentally sensitive province of British Columbia, Canada, where she puts her concern for her mountain home into action. Here is her moment of change:

About two weeks before November 20, 2014, I began to hear about protestors on Burnaby Mountain. I live on Burnaby Mountain, so this piqued my interest. I was on leave from work and I thought it would be a good use of my time to go learn about what was going on in my community *and why the protesters had set up camp on the mountain.*

Kinder Morgan (now Trans Mountain) was trying to bore some test holes for a tunnel that would move dilbit through the mountain. The pipeline that they were hoping to build would begin in Edmonton (my hometown) and come to an end in Burnaby (where I live now). The dilbit is a very cheap and dirty oil, and Trans Mountain's plan was to add a whole bunch of chemicals to it so that it can flow through the pipeline to be put into tankers and shipped to China.

I sat in the camp with my sister, at the sacred fire with another pair of sisters who were Elders in their community. The first fact I learned was that these people were not "protestors." They are Protectors with deep commitment to Earth and to water. "Water is life" is the second truth that was shared with me.

I learned that this movement is Indigenous-led and that the pipeline, Site C Dam, and all the invasive projects that were being proposed and built were on unceded Indigenous territory. That means that this land was never fought over or signed over to the

Canadian government. In its most simple form, this land is Indigenous, and they are the natural and historical stewards of this land.

I learned more about Amnesty International's report, "No More Stolen Sisters," and how these pipeline projects and missing Indigenous girls and women are related. I learned of the environmental issues related to a pipeline running from Edmonton to less than 1 km from my house. I was horrified to learn that I live within the "blast zone" of the tank farm. If anything serious goes wrong *with that pipeline*, my home is in danger.

To be fair, I didn't learn everything I need to know at the camp or in the sanctuary. I did make a promise to the fire-keepers that I would do whatever I could to protect the sacred fire, and I did my best. We all did. And then the Royal Canadian Mounted Police moved in.

I remember someone yelling "link your arms and get him in the centre," so we did. We surrounded and protected an Indigenous man; I think my back was to him. We were singing warrior songs and our supporters sang with us. Then the RCMP started removing people quite forcefully, one by one, until I was the last one. My husband called me the Last Warrior. My heart was pounding. As I sat there, waiting, people were taking pictures and video and flashing me the peace sign and saying they loved me. I was waiting. One of the Indigenous fire-keepers started drumming for me, and this incredible thing happened. I started looking around at the forest, which is my home, and I was looking at the sun dappling through the leaves, and as I was noticing the moss and the ferns and all the beauty around me and smelling the rotting, gorgeous, loamy smell, I listened, and I could not hear any birds. That's one thing on this mountain, you will always hear birds, there are so many, but I couldn't hear any birds. I thought to myself:

If Kinder Morgan comes in here, this mountain won't hear birds anymore, they won't see the bears anymore, the coyotes won't "woo-oo-wow at night." All these wonderful living beings that ARE the mountain would be decimated.

All of a sudden, I could feel an energy swirling around me. It started like a breeze at first and slowly gained strength. It was a vortex moving straight through my hips up into my spine, around and through my heart. Then I could feel a similar current swirling around my third eye, down to my mind, to my heart, down into the earth. The two whirlpools of energy combined until they were a double helix in my soul. That's the moment when I realized my life was different. Vastly different. The mountain spirit that some call "apu" spoke to me in a language stronger than words. My work was to protect Earth and all water. At that moment I became a different Sparrow. This became my mountain to protect. Not my mountain in the way that I might own it, but my mountain to love and adore. My heart, my eyes, and my mind were opened. The date was November 20, 2014.

For days I had been telling my sister that if anything "went down" I was going to go with the flow. I was preparing to do the right thing. I was finally prepared. All my life I had been working up to this.

I am a settler; my mom was a settler. Both of my mom's husbands are Indigenous. Therefore, I grew up in an Indigenous home. Most of my early childhood memories are of being at sweats, ball tournaments, powwows, visiting Elders, and learning Cree. My dad is a spiritual man. At least he was; I haven't seen him for a long time. He taught us how to be with Spirit and to listen. He taught us about Creator (and even told us that Creator could be a woman). Dad taught us many things. Mom was no slouch either.

At the same time Dad was teaching us traditional values and spirituality, mom was teaching us about the Goddess. Mama was a goddess-worshipper from the time she could think for herself. To be honest, it probably started with Mary worship, but that's okay. Between the two of them I have a strong relationship with Spirit and with Earth.

It wasn't a split-second decision to be in that place at that time. It was a decision that was coming for many years. In that moment I too become a "protector" and I am proud of the decision that I made that day. I will keep fighting these devasting projects that only hurt our Mother and ourselves.

Sparrow Kemp

• • • •

Affirm Your Connection

Not everyone will be so lucky as to have a moment of connection to the earth like Sparrow did. It was a life-changing moment that has had a profound effect on her and has gifted her with the privilege of being able to pinpoint her exact moment of awakening to the power of the earth.

In times of crisis, what do you really believe in? The earth is constant, reliable, and eternal. Even a person with no spiritual or religious leanings can sense that. Grant yourself permission to be open to the subtle messages that the earth sends. Watch for the patterns that are inherent in the seasons, the migration of animals, and weather patterns, and challenge yourself to act accordingly

Since the first human scratched an image on the wall of a cave, we have been marking and defining our sacred spaces. We have built sacred sites and temples, and created groups and institutions to bring us together on a quest to organize, document, and categorize our natural world and our spiritual experiences. With so much of the ancient history of witchcraft and paganism being lost to the mists of time, it has become extremely important for many modern practitioners to ensure this does not happen again by collecting and recording the recent history of the movement and this is something that everyone can participate in.

Write Your Own Story

Keeping a journal is a very personal and private way to ensure that your own story is not lost, and that you have a document to look back on to chart your spiritual growth and reflections along the way. I have a stack of notebooks, some dedicated to topics such as recipes, herbalism, and notes from lectures or workshops I have attended, and yet another stack dedicated to particular parts of my training in the Witchcraft traditions I participate in. My coven also has a journal. We make an entry for every meeting we have, detailing who attended, what we did, magic worked, and relevant seasonal or lunar information. This comes in handy when we want to follow up on a piece of magic or remember who was involved in an event or class. It can be inspiring, and occasionally hilarious, to look back and remember what we were thinking and doing at any given time.

We live in an incredible time, so close to the genesis of the modern Witchcraft movement. We have the technology to be able to communicate with some of the people who were involved in the very early days, or at least people who knew the people who were around when things were just getting underway. Neopaganism as we know it exploded into the mainstream less than one hundred years ago, and this gives each of us a part to play in actively shaping how our communities will be moving forward. As earthy as these paths may be, they are not carved in stone. We can adapt them and mold them to serve us and honour the traditions of the past.

Chapter 2

MYTHOLOGICAL EARTH BEASTS AND PLACES

The mythical creatures associated with the earth element fall into very specific categories:

1. Beings that personify the natural landscape
2. Beings that dwell in an earth-related place such as a cave, rock, mountain, or tree
3. Beings that perform some kind of domestic service, such as protecting a place or doing manual labour
4. Beings that form or become the landscape

Bluecap: In English folklore, these are fairies or spirits that dwell in mines. They appear as a blue flame and warn miners of cave-ins. They are incredibly strong and are very hard workers. But they don't work for free; they expect their pay just like the rest of the miners. Their wages must be left in a corner of the mine every payday. If you try to shortchange them, they ignore the insult and leave the money alone. If you pay them extra, they only take the money they fairly earned. Related mine spirits called *coblynau* exist in Wales. In Cornwall the knockers warn of cave-ins; they appear in the United States as tommyknockers.

Brownie: Native to Britain, these fairies are helpful household creatures who come out at night to do domestic chores while everyone else is asleep. They require no compensation aside from some nice fresh cream and some tidbits of fine food. These offerings prevent them from turning tricksy and causing trouble around the house.

Dryad: These beautiful female nature spirits from Greek mythology are the nymphs that inhabit trees, groves, and woodlands. They are related to the Hamadryads, who are specific to trees and only live as long as the tree does. Originally Dryads were the designated nymphs of oak trees, but the name became a catch-all for woodland spirts. There are other types of Dryads that correspond with specific trees, such as the *Meliai* of the ash trees, the *Daphniae* of the laurel trees, and the *Pteleai* of elm trees.

Dwarves: In Germanic and Scandinavian folklore, dwarves are the short, stout master craftsmen that dwell underground and inside mountains. They are known for their long beards and wizened appearance and are quite often seen as being blackened by the dirt and grit from living underground. Dwarves are extremely talented at blacksmithing and crafting beautiful objects out of precious metals and gems. The mighty hammer of the god Thor, called Mjollnir, and the goddess Freya's beautiful necklace, the Brisingamen, were made by the dwarves. They are tribal creatures, with different groups having their own kings, territories, and leaders. They build elaborately decorated great halls and tunnel systems to live and store their treasures in. A dwarf can be temperamental, rising quickly to anger and always ready for a good fight, but easily subdued with good food and drink. They possess occult and magical knowledge, the power of invisibility, and deep wisdom in the nature of the earth.

Gargoyle: These stone guardians adorn classic buildings and have two distinct purposes: their bodies form a conduit to direct rainwater from the roof, and their intimidating appearances ward off evil spirits. The Notre Dame Cathedral in Paris is renowned for its collection of gargoyles dating back to medieval times. The use of gargoyles as architectural features dates back to ancient Egypt as well as Greece and Rome. The earliest known example is in Turkey and dates back thirteen thousand years. The most familiar forms of gargoyle blend animal, monster, and human features to create a frightening hybrid figure. Similar figures that do not serve as rain gutters are simply called grotesques and are decorative as well as being handy at keeping evil away.

Giants: Stories of giant human-like beings with supernatural powers appear in many cultures. Gog and Magog are mythical giants and are celebrated as the traditional guardians of the city of London. Norse legends speak of a race of giants, or Jötunns, that were the first living beings and lived in Jotunheim, a wild land of dense forests, high mountains, ice, and rock. It was from the dead body of the giant Ymir that the gods created the worlds. Impressive land masses are sometimes seen as being the sleeping or dead bodies of deified giants. "The Sleeping Giant," found near Thunder Bay, Ontario, is said to be the body of Nanabijou, a benevolent spirit of the local Ojibwa people. Nanabijou lay down in the waters of Lake Superior and turned to stone in order to protect a valuable silver mine from white settlers, after its secret location was revealed by greed and trickery. From the shore, you can clearly see the outline of a giant lying on his back, arms folded across his chest.

Gnome: These small humanoid earth-dwelling beings are the personification of the earth itself. The popular image of the gnome appears in gardens, made of plastic and wearing a pointed red cap and wide grin. This is a reference to the gnome's close connection to nature and their natural inclination toward tending and protecting earth's resources. Sixteenth-century alchemist and philosopher Paracelsus introduced gnomes as the elemental being of earth. There are many types of gnomes and they are found in forests, gardens, houses, and underground. They can pass through the solid forms of their realms as easily as a fish swims in water.

Goblin: These beings look somewhat like gnomes but have a more ragged and scary appearance, and they tend to be malevolent and malicious. They like to cause trouble and play nasty pranks on people. They may wake up a household by banging on the walls or smashing pots and pans together in the middle of the night. These are not to be confused with hobgoblins, which are just mischievous, lacking the nastiness of the goblin.

Golem: This figure from Jewish folklore is a human figure made of clay and then brought to life by way of a magical charm written on paper and placed in the effigy's mouth. The golem then became a protector to the person who animated them, or to the Jewish people as a group.

Hobbits: In the world of Middle-Earth, as described by J. R. R. Tolkien, hobbits are "a little people, about half our height and smaller than bearded dwarves." They live in subterranean houses, called hobbit-holes, which they equip with all the comforts of home—good food, the finest wine and ale, abundant pipe-weed, and all the most comfortable domestic accoutrements. They prefer to stick close to the comforts of home, rarely leaving their Shire to go on adventures, but when they do ...

Menninkäinen: A forest being from Finnish folklore. They are hard-working and fond of riddles. They resemble a leprechaun in that if you manage to catch one, they will grant you a wish. They have evolved from being seen as spirits of the dead in early folklore to being seen more like a gnome or goblin in modern interpretations.

Nisse: These Scandinavian domestic spirits stand no taller than a toddler, but they are easily as strong as a large full-grown man. They are domestic guardians and helpers that take care of the house, farm, and associated family. The nisse have a good sense of humour and like practical jokes. But this can go terribly wrong if they are not respected and appeased with good things to eat and drink, especially at Christmas. The tomte is a Swedish relative of the nisse.

Nymph: In Greek mythology nymphs are a class of nature spirits that includes Oreads (mountain spirits), Dryads (trees, groves, woodlands), Meliae (flowers), Naiads (fresh water), and Nereids (the sea). They appear as lovely young women and they are seductive and beguiling, often having affairs with gods and mortals alike. The tutelary deity of the nymphs is Artemis, goddess of vegetation, wild animals, hunting, and childbirth.

Otso: In Finland, Otso is the archetypal spirit of bears. It is taboo to speak directly of the bear, so many epithets are used instead: King of the Forest, Honeypaws, and Fur-Robed Forest Friend are a few.

Sasquatch: In the northwest of Canada and the United States, the legend of an upright-walking ape-like creature living in the deepest forests has been handed down for generations. The stories originate from pre-colonial Indigenous beliefs. The name Sasquatch is taken from the Salish word *Sasq'ets*, which means "wild man." Also known as Bigfoot, it is thought to be somehow related to the Himalayan yeti (see below).

Satyr: These half-beast, half-man creatures come from Greek mythology and were the companions of the god of wine, Dionysus. Satyrs have the hooves and horns of a goat or a ram and the head and upper body of a human male, and are depicted in art as sporting an erect phallus and carrying a cup of wine or a musical instrument. They roam the woodlands, enjoying music, intoxicants, and the company of nymphs. Their Roman counterparts are known as fauns.

Yeti: These great shaggy ape-men are much like the Sasquatch of North America. They are said to live in the Himalayan mountains at very high altitudes. They are folkloric characters in the stories of the Sherpa people, who tell the stories to warn against the dangers that abound in the mountains.

Mythological Places

Around the world, tales of lost lands, eternal paradises, and supernatural homes are common themes. Whether they physically existed or not is irrelevant, because they have such a strong presence in the folklore and psyche of the cultures that speak of them. The stories of these places teach and inspire us just as much as any actual physical place would. This list gives some examples of such places, and what they represent:

Axis Mundi: This is the central point of the world around which all of creation revolves. It is the place where the upper world (realm of spirit), the middle world (our material realm), and the lower world (realm of the dead and the supernatural) are connected. The way they are connected can take the form of a human construction such as a temple or a monument, or it could be a natural feature like a mountain or a tree. Yggdrasil, the Norse Tree of Life, is an axis mundus, with its roots reaching down into the earth, its branches extending into the sky and its trunk connecting the two.

Cockaigne: The mythical land of Cockaigne was a sensory pleasure paradise where gluttony, sloth, and indulgence in luxury and comfort was the order of the day. Sex was free and the rivers flowed with wine and honey. This utopian fantasy was popular across Europe during the Middle Ages, and versions of the story were recorded in many languages. Many of the tales depicted Cockaigne as an ideal world for peasants and serfs, and a perfect daydream to escape the drudgery of their everyday lives.

El Dorado: Spanish conquistadors in the sixteenth century heard rumors that a lost city of gold existed somewhere in South America and they set out on several expeditions to find it. They were eventually followed by English adventurers and an era of greed, conquest, and colonization ensued. The legendary city was never found, but the name still stands as a euphemism for a land of treasure and extraordinary wealth.

Garden of Eden: This biblical garden is described in the book of Genesis as the earthly paradise that Adam and Eve lived in until they disobeyed God and were expelled. It is included in the creation stories of three of the world's main religions, the Jewish, Muslim, and Christian faiths. Over the centuries many theories have been suggested on where the Garden of Eden could have been located. In the Bible, four rivers flowing in the garden were named and two of them, the Tigris and the Euphrates, still exist; some believe that the garden may be lost under the waters of the Persian Gulf. A second theory suggests that the garden was lost forever during the Great Flood, and yet another idea suggest that it may not have been on Earth at all but existed somewhere in the heavens.

Garden of the Hesperides: The Hesperides were the nymphs of evening and sunsets who tended the garden where the goddess Hera kept her golden apple trees. Hera received the trees from Gaia as a wedding gift when she married Zeus. Eating a golden apple would grant immortality, and their colour was thought to give the golden light to sunsets.

Hanging Gardens of Babylon: Of the Seven Wonders of the Ancient World, the Hanging Gardens of Babylon is the only one that has yet to be proven to have actually existed. Legend has it that King Nebuchadnezzar II built these fantastical gardens to adorn the city of Babylon sometime around the sixth century BCE. The gardens were said to be planted on a huge, terraced brick structure. The plantings draped over the sides to give the appearance of hanging. Accounts written by classical writers describe elaborate irrigation systems and a structure nearly five stories tall. It would have been a wonder indeed to keep a garden thriving in Babylon's desert climate. No remains of the gardens have ever been verified, so these writers and artists' drawings are the only evidence that remain, and some of these are suspect as they were created long after the gardens were said to exist.

Middle World: Practitioners of earth-based traditions will refer to the Upper, Middle, and Lower Worlds to describe three different levels of reality. Using techniques such as meditation or journeying, the practitioner can "travel" to these places to communicate with and learn from the entities that live there. The Upper World is the realm of the deities; the Lower World is where the dead and supernatural entities live. The Middle

World is our material realm where we live. This is the realm in which you can journey to commune with the spirits of the things you can see in your everyday life—plants, animals, places, rocks, and water, for example. You may encounter the spirit of a recently deceased person who has not yet crossed over to their afterlife yet. Developing the skill to access the Middle World this way gives you access to very practical earth-based energy for solving problems, getting spiritual support, and working magic.

Midgard: One of the nine worlds from Norse myth, Midgard is the actual physical realm in which we live. It was created by the gods from the slain body of the giant Ymir (Aurgelmir). They used his flesh to create the land, made the mountains from his bones, and his blood became the waters.

Tír na nÓg: In the mythology of Ireland, Tir na nÓg is the land out in the western sea that can only be accessed by means of magic. It is known as a kind of paradise and land of eternal youth, peace, happiness, and comfort. It is inhabited by the mythical Tuatha dé Danann, (People of the Goddess Danu) who were said to be driven out of Ireland by the Milesians, the people who came before the Celtic people of Ireland. Tir na nÓg is an otherworld, which means that it can be visited by living humans, if they can find the means to get there.

Sherwood Forest: This location has the distinction of being both real and mythical. The real Sherwood Forest is in Nottingham-shire, England, and covers 375 hectares of land. It is a primarily oak forest, with more than one thousand ancient oaks, including the thousand-year-old Major Oak, which is said to have been the meeting place for the mythic hero, Robin Hood, and his band of Merry Men.

Summerland: In some Wiccan and Wicca-influenced traditions, Summerland is seen as the place where the spirits of the dead go to rest and renew before they are reincarnated. As the name implies, it is a land where summer is eternal, and nature is pristine. Some see it as being across the seas, to the west, where it is represented by the setting of the sun. It is not a heaven, nor is it a hell, as it has neither a positive nor a negative connotation; it is seen as a neutral resting place. Particular lore may vary depending on the tradition, and some Wiccans may not include Summerland in their tradition at all.

• • • •

Family

Some land spirits and mythical creatures are indigenous to the land, and some are brought along with the settlers that came from other countries, as supernatural immigrants. The following essay describes what honouring both native and naturalized land sprits can look like.

Austin Lawrence is known as "Auz" to kith and kin. He is the one of the Stewards of Raven's Knoll, a rural campground and event centre established for Canada's Pagan communities. He is also an inclusive Heathen goði. Auz works for Public Safety Canada and is a doctoral candidate studying right-wing extremism and Germanic Neopaganism.

MY FATHER'S FAMILY are from Anglo-Saxon settlers who have been in North America since the time of the Puritan landings. My mother's family immigrated to Canada from Denmark. Growing up, I was socialized as a secular humanist; our spirituality was experiencing nature on wilderness canoe trips or encountering the wonderful diversity of humanity through travelling Earth. In my teens, I got interested in religions because I wondered, "What enchantment was missing from my worldview?" In my adulthood, I settled upon Heathenry, specifically Ásatrú with a bit of Anglo-Saxon Paganism thrown in for good measure. Looking back on my childhood, the most "religious" feelings I had were experienced during the Yuletide. Our Yule traditions drew heavily upon the "secular" Danish Christmas traditions, which are actually more like a combination of antiquarian Pagan reconstructions and folkloric Heathen survivals. The Yule is a time of ancestral remembrance, gifting, olden songs, Heathen symbols, gratitude, blessings, and good cheer.

The ancient Germanic Heathens had a legal concept for ancient family-held land, called "odal" land (O.N. óðal; O.E. ēþel). This land was held in common by an extended family-clan called an "ættir." The connection of the people to their land was a sacred bond that could not even be broken by a king. The relationship was affirmed through the rite of interring one's dead on the land, in barrow mounds. The living would offer at these mounds to their ancestors, ensuring the cycle of gift-giving would continue. In Heathen theology, relational gifting is what weaves peoples and worlds together. It is through offerings that gratitude is given, and blessings are sought. It is how peace, fecundity, and good fortune are forged. In our religion, the gifting of offerings is both a metaphor and a driver of similar cycles in both the human and natural worlds, the cycles of the seasons, and of nature.

After centuries, the ancestor in the mound would be forgotten. Sometimes people moved to a new country and found mysterious ancient mounds already there. In either instance, the figure of the mound-dwelling ancestor evolved to become a numinous elf (O.N. álfar) or magical dwarf (O.N. dvergr): a supernatural species, cognate to humanity, that was also created at the start of time by the gods, but set to dwell in the underworlds as neighbours to the human dead. After the first wave of Christianity eradicated traces of Heathen religion through demonization, the next phase of domination was the process of diminution. What remaining Pagan rites and beliefs that were not completely suppressed were transformed into quaint superstitions. Yet, while it seemed that Abrahamic monotheist thinking had thoroughly colonized the mind of Germanic peoples, elements of the Pagan past still survived. People still told their versions of the old stories and practiced the old rites of leaving out gifts of offerings, maybe not to the old gods, but at least to the remaining little "hidden people" (O.N. huldufólk) who now stood for them, in the same places.

A "nisse" is a sort of Danish household spirit, originally a spirt of the farmstead. Some believe that the word is derived from the Old Norse word *niðsi*, with the meaning of "dear little relative." The view that this spirit replaced the ancestral odal mound spirit is further clarified by the synonyms found for this figure in other parts of Scandinavia; with names that translate as "homestead man," "yard fellow," "farm guardian," "mound man," "barrow farmer," and the like. They are the secret guardians of hearths, outbuildings (like the brewing and dairying rooms), barns, fields, and gardens, as well as all who depend on them, whether they be animal or person.

A nisse is often imagined as a knee-high old man with a full beard, a woolen tunic, a stout belt, breeches, and often with a tall pointed red hat. They are as strong as a full-grown adult person, are very hard workers, and are sticklers for fairness. If you treat your nisse well, by talking to them often, not destroying places they frequent (like their mound), and feeding them the porridge, butter, cream, or other things they love so much, your household will have good fortune. However, this may not always be enough. If you are greedy, if you mistreat animals, if you eliminate all wild

42

vegetation on your property or cut down too many trees, or if you do not follow the principles of kindness and social justice with those that live in your household or those guests that visit it ... well, you might find your beer or milk soured, or your keys or phone missing, or your knife might slip to give you a bad cut, or a non-functioning smoke alarm might cause a house fire. How does this happen? Well, nisse are masters of illusion. They can shape-shift into things like a black cat or an impoverished elderly traveller. They can glamour humans with illusions, specializing in turning themselves or objects invisible for a time. They also don't mind if their educational pranks teach you a harsh lesson.

My wife and I purchased land for the use of Canada's Pagan communities about a decade ago. It is here that Canada's largest Pagan event takes place, the Kaleidoscope Gathering, as well as numerous other events by hedge witches, Wiccans, Druids, Heathens, and every other flavour of Neopaganism. When we first came to Raven's Knoll, we discovered a small mound in a quiet area of the forest, under the towering white pine forest. I immediately felt like this was a place for the nisse. I took three stones and created a tiny doorway into the mound, which made it look much like a passage grave. In the blackness, in that little burrow, was the underworld. I had found and created the same form as those large mounds that migrating ancients recognize as sacred sites, at which they would offer to "those who were before": the elves, the dead, the *aes sídhe*, the fairy-folk, the *jogahoh*, the *land-vættir*, the land-wights, the *awwakkulé*, the little people, the *canotila*, the trows, and many more. For, in our tradition, this is where the local spirits of the land reside.

I added two tiny statues of gnomes that looked like nisse on either side of the doorway. Through my first offering of shiny silver coins, cream, and honey, I communed with the nisse. With this first offering, I spoke about how glad I was that nisse came to this new place with me, that I was happy they could introduce me to the other hidden folk of this locale, and that I was glad to enter into a relationship with them. I left cedar, sweet grass, tobacco, and buffalo sage for these new hidden friends, as is the custom of my wife's Indigenous ancestors and the ancestors of the First Peoples of the Ottawa Valley. I spoke about how we would behave with virtue and kindness to the best of our abilities, how we would be good stewards of the land, and of our hope that the nisse would keep people at Raven's Knoll safe from accident or misfortune. I spoke about how my ancestors' bodies had become dirt and grown into the new life of my family, grown into the plants, forests, and animals of the very land. I spoke about how my people and the nisse had moved over long distances and time, but that we both still held on to the old ways. Like the nisse, our tradition has value even if it is no longer the biggest religion, even if secular truths mute the mysteries, even if we only have simple infrastructure, even if we are not protected by the shield of the powerful. Though demonized, though diminutized, we Heathens are still here. We still know that a gift deserves a gift.

Austin Lawrence

• • • •

The Land Is Alive

Myths and legends of fantastical creatures and places are found wherever you go on Earth. The lore of ancestral homelands migrated with people as they settled new parts of the globe and the stories of local beings and places shift and change as new generations are born. I personally like to think that these legends are rooted in some kernel of truth, that somewhere back in time a real being or place inspired the folktales and beliefs of a given culture.

I would also like to think that, generations from now, our descendants will be telling amazing stories of the legendary Raven's Knoll and its mound inhabited by nisse and the spirits of the rowdy pagans that have camped nearby.

Chapter 3

EARTH AND THE DIVINE

The element of earth is set apart from the other elements of fire, water, and air in that it has been deified in a universal way, globally and throughout time. Even in the secular world, it is common to hear the term "Mother Earth" used to describe our planet.

Throughout the myths and stories of the Earth Goddess archetype are themes of creation, fertility, birth, death, abundance, and destruction. In many cultures the goddess is the earth and is partnered with a sky god. Together they create the heavens, the world, and all of life.

Many earth deities are inextricably linked to the earthy pursuits of agriculture, hunting, and fertility. These basic human concerns needed to be successful in order to ensure that the people would thrive. In every early culture, methods of petitioning and appeasing these higher powers became part of the seasonal festivals and everyday customs of life. The mysteries of sprouting seeds, childbirth, harvesting, finding game, and raising healthy livestock were attributed to divine influence, and all these aspects of life were seen to have overseeing matron and patron deities that would decide who and what would be fruitful.

Fertility gods and goddesses for the sake of farming and hunting was one thing, but for the fertility of humans, it was a much more serious matter. Until the rise of modern medicine, the difficult, dangerous, and sometimes fatal act of childbirth lent urgent need for divine protection. Women regularly died giving birth to their babies, and the mortality rate for newborns was much higher than it is now. Earth deities, such as the Slavic Mokosh, were sought for the protection of birthing mothers. Prayers and offerings to such protectors were made in hopes of a safe, healthy birth and speedy recovery for the mother and child.

Gods and goddesses can also be linked to one specific part of the earth, or some attribute of it. Regional deities such as the Cailleach of the Gaelic speaking parts of Britain are said to be responsible for creating many of the area's mountains and hills, as well as being connected to many burial mounds and standing stones.

Our language also indicates an inclination toward a familial relationship to the land. When we speak of the place we call home, we use words like "motherland" and "fatherland" to indicate our attachment to it. The country that we came from or that our ancestors emigrated from is called our "mother country."

☺⁄☺

Angela Grey is a Wiccan priestess, poet, and avid nature lover. Born and raised in Yukon Territory, she has lived in communities across Canada and has a deep connection to the land.

Invocation to the Cailleach

(start softly)
I call to the bringer of storms
I call to the frost-bearer, the blue-faced hag
To She who stirs the cauldron at Coryvrekan
I call to the grey-veiled walker in the night.
(with rising volume)
I call to the howling voice in the gale:
Stone Striker!
Wolf Rider!
Mountain Maker!
To the hand that wields the creel and hammer,
And shapes the hills with thunder!
Cailleach!
Eldest!
Mother of Winter!
I call you by your ancient names
So that I may honour you!

Angela Grey

• • • •

Deities of Earth

Ala *(Nigerian)*: Earth goddess associated with fertility of humans and animals. Ala ensures that babies grow in their mother's womb, and watches over them as the mature. As ruler of the underworld, she receives the dead into her own body, the earth.

Asase Ya *(West African)*: Earth goddess who is associated with fields and the fertility of the land. She is married to Nyame, god of the sky, and is mother to the trickster Anansi. Her sacred day is Thursday, the day the earth was created.

Bes *(Egyptian)*: Patron god of households, childbirth, and fertility, possibly of Nubian origin. Depicted as a short, squat, bearded dwarf, statues of Bes were used to guard the households of ancient Egyptians from misfortune.

Cailleach *(Celtic)*: Known throughout Scotland, Ireland, and the Isle of Man as a creator goddess and bringer of storms. She is said to create the landscape from the rocks she carries in her apron. Her name translates to "hag," "old woman," and "veiled one." Her legend is tied to more geographical locations in Britain than any other Celtic deity.

Cernunnos *(Celtic)*: One of the most beloved gods of the Neo-pagan movement, he is a horned god, associated with animals, abundance, nature, and the wild. Very little is known about this deity, as there are no historic myths or stories about him. There are images of this horned deity that have been found in areas of Europe that had been inhabited by the Celts, the most famous of which is the image of a seated figure holding a torc and a snake, surrounded by wild animals. This is found on the Gundestrup Cauldron, a large ceremonial vessel that was excavated from a peat bog in Denmark in 1891.

Cybele *(Greek)*: Earth goddess of nature, caves, fertility, and mountains. Referred to as "Mother of the Gods," she is often depicted with leopards, the animal that is said to have raised her when she was an orphaned child. She was called Magna Mater by her devotees in ancient Rome, and her frenzied Roman male followers, called *Galli*, were known to ritually castrate themselves, adopt female dress, and lead wild celebrations with music, dancing, drinking, and drumming.

Demeter *(Greek)*: Goddess of fertility, the cycle of life and death, and agriculture. A devoted mother, she caused famine for the people of Greece when she went searching for her daughter Persephone, who had been kidnapped by Hades and taken to the underworld. She is associated with vegetation and crops, most notably grain. Her sacred animals are the pig and the snake.

Danu *(Celtic)*: This mysterious goddess is the mother of the Tuatha Dé Danann (Children of Danu), the ancient tribe of beings that inhabited Ireland in prehistory. Very little lore has been recorded about Danu, but she is considered to be an earth goddess and bestower of all wisdom, knowledge, abundance, magic, and fertility to her descendants and to the land.

Diana *(Roman)*: Goddess of hunting, wilderness, fertility, women, and witchcraft. Common depictions of Diana illustrate her as beautiful, in motion, carrying a bow and arrow, in mid-hunt. She is accompanied by wild animals, usually a stag, and is a guardian of the forests. Over time she evolved to also become a lunar goddess. She is the mother of Aradia, the goddess of the witches.

Dionysus *(Greek)*: A nature god of wine, vegetation, and ecstasy. His epithet is "God of the Vine," and he was known in ancient

Rome as Bacchus. Conceived by a mortal mother, Semele, and the great god Zeus, he was the last god to arrive at Mount Olympus. He travelled the earth teaching humans about wine and inspiring art, literature, and great orgiastic rites.

Dumuzi *(Sumerian)*: God of crops, harvest, and vegetation. He is referred to as "The Shepherd." Linked to the death and rebirth cycle of the green and growing things on earth, he spends half the year in the underworld, creating winter, and half the year on earth granting summer.

Epona *(Celtic)*: Fertility goddess and mother goddess figure, strongly associated with horses. Her worship was adopted by Roman cavalry during the occupation of Britain and was carried with the soldiers all the way back to Rome, where shrines to her have been found. Ancient sculptures often depict her sitting astride a horse and holding a basket of fruit or a cornucopia.

Gaia *(Greek)*: Earth goddess. Alternate spelling Gaea. She is the Mother of all creation and personification of planet Earth. She emerged out of Chaos and gave birth to Uranus, who was the personification of the Sky. Together they gave life to the twelve Titans who ruled the universe before the Olympians. She was also the mother of several other offspring, including the three Fates, the Hecantoncheires, and numerous Meliades, cyclops, and giants.

Geb *(Egyptian)*: An earth god also known as Keb or Seb. Along with his wife and sister, the sky goddess Nut, he was the father to Seth, Isis, and Osiris. He is often depicted in a prone position, personifying the earth, with Nut arching above him. His sacred animal is the goose, and he is said to have laid a great egg that represented rebirth and renewal. He is credited with creating the gems and precious minerals extracted from the earth and is also the god of mines and caves.

Hestia *(Greek)*: Goddess of home and hearth and one of the twelve Olympians. Daughter of Cronus and Rhea, she chose to remain a virgin, and declined proposals from Apollo and Poseidon. She presides over all domestic life and her key symbol is the hearth fire. She is graceful and modest, benevolent, and patient; she teaches us domestic management and hospitality. Her Roman equivalent is Vesta.

Isis *(Egyptian)*: An all-encompassing goddess of earth, motherhood, and fertility. She is considered a role model for all women and the ultimate mother figure. In art she is often depicted nursing the baby Horus, her child with Osiris. When Osiris died it was the tears of Isis that caused the flooding of the Nile and brought fertility to the delta. As a healer she is capable of curing the sick and bringing the dead back to life. She arose from being a relatively minor deity to being one of the most revered deities in Egypt. Her influence grew, and in time it spread throughout the Roman Empire and beyond. Her worship continues to this day.

Izanami *(Japanese)*: Primordial Shinto goddess of creation and the underworld. Her name translates to "She Who Invites." In partnership with her husband, the god Izanagi ("He Who Invites"), she created the islands of Japan and gave birth to several of the other Shinto deities. They are depicted in traditional art as standing together on the bridge between heaven and earth, stirring the waters of the ocean with a spear. According to the creation myth, salt from the water crystalized on the jeweled spear tip and, upon falling back into the ocean, formed islands.

Jord *(Norse)*: Earth goddess reputed to be a giantess and the mother of the god Thor. Her name translates to "Earth."

Mielikki *(Finnish)*: Goddess of forests. In exchange for praising her beauty, hunters would receive a successful hunt. She has the power to heal injured animals, and she played a key role in the creation of bears. Both she and her forest god husband Tapio can shape-shift into bears.

Mokosh *(Slavic)*: Revered as the personification of the moist mother earth, and married to Perun, the dry sky god. She is associated with fertility and childbirth as well as spinning and weaving. She is known to take the shape of stones.

Nerthus *(Germanic)*: Earth goddess revered by several tribes including the Angles, who later invaded Britain. The Roman historian Tacitus wrote an account of her worship around 100 BCE, in which he claimed that on an island in the Baltic Sea was a temple dedicated to Nerthus. A statue of her would be veiled and set on a cart that was drawn by cows. The cart would process around the communities and, while this was happening, there was celebrating, and all weapons and hostility would be set aside. Upon her return to her temple, the statue and cart would be washed by slaves in a sacred lake, and then the slaves would be drowned as sacrifice. Tacitus regarded her as Terra Mater, Mother Earth.

Pachamama *(Andean)*: A supreme Mother Earth goddess honoured by the Indigenous people of the Andes mountains in Peru, Bolivia, and Argentina. As a creator she oversees plants, animals, fertility, and agriculture. She will also destroy and cause earthquakes when she is disrespected.

Pan *(Greek)*: The wild and irrepressible half-man, half-goat god of nature, pastures, flocks, wild woods, and music. Born in Arcadia to the god Hermes and a Dryad, Pan wanders through wild and lonely places, playing his panpipes and indulging in legendary sexuality by chasing nymphs.

Prithvi *(Hindu)*: Earth goddess known as "The Vast One." Her name is the Sanskrit word for earth. She is married to the sky god Dyaus, and together they are worshipped as the parents of the other gods. Nurturing, maternal, and supportive, Prithvi's epithets include "Nursing Mother," "Mother of Plants," and "Source of Everything." Her sacred animal is the cow.

Sif *(Norse)*: An earth goddess associated with wheat, fertility, and family. Wife of Thor, she was renowned for her beautiful, cascading, long golden hair, which is thought to represent the wheat crops of the people. Her hair was cut off by the trickster Loki, and her tears flooded the land, destroying the crops. Thor forced Loki to find a way to replace Sif's hair. Loki went to visit the Gnomes, who made Sif a cap with hair of spun gold thread, which enabled Sif to once again help the people with their crops.

Tellus *(Roman)*: Earth Goddess, also known as Terra Mater. She presided over fecundity, marriage, and procreation. She was later conflated with the Greek Cybele.

Tlaltechutli *(Aztec)*: A fearsome earth goddess whose name means "The one who gives and devours life," a moniker earned by her need for blood sacrifice. Possessing both female and male qualities, Tlaltechutli is thought to be dual gender, but is more commonly portrayed in female form.

Umay/Umai *(Turkic)*: An Earth Mother type goddess of fertility and children. She watches over the act of childbirth and is also the protector of the household.

Veles *(Slavic)*: An earth god, he is also referred to as Volos and Lord of the Forest. He appears in the shape of a bear, but has the power to shapeshift into other animal forms. He is the protector of wild animals and the warrior who will defend them, and the forest.

Xipe Totec *(Aztec)*: God of agricultural fertility. His name means "Our Lord with flayed skin," a reference to the death of the old vegetation and the growth of the new.

Bringing Them In

Calling on an entity for a ritual or magical working usually comes in one of two ways: you invoke them, or you evoke them. The words tend to get used interchangeably, but they do have different meanings and very different results. Both practices manifest the deity in our world, give them a place on earth, and give us an opportunity to interact with them in a tangible and intimate, physical way.

To invoke an entity is to call on them, and invite them directly into your body, allowing them to possess you. To evoke an entity is to call on them to be present, but not to enter your body. Both practices are common in many Pagan and Witchcraft traditions, and it is helpful to understand the mechanics of each action.

Entities that may be called include deities, elemental beings, nature spirits, and even the spirits of beloved dead or ancestors.

Before you attempt to evoke or invoke an entity, be clear on your purpose for doing so. Some common reasons may include:

- A devotional ritual to honour that particular entity
- To petition it for a favour
- To have it bear witness to your ritual, and lend support and/or guidance
- To aid in some form of divination
- To provide messages from the deceased

Evocation

For most purposes, evoking a deity, element, or spirit is the most appropriate way to go. This requires some thought and preparation, but it does not require the level of practice, training, or risk that invoking an entity does. You can be successful evoking an entity just using your words, but it can be very meaningful and helpful to add in some ritual actions, such as lighting a candle and giving an offering. Lighting some incense works well as an offering. The fragrance can be enjoyed by entities regardless of whether they have a material form or not. The inclusion of these simple ritual actions provides an evocative atmosphere, and they have been performed by countless practitioners over time. They are universally recognizable as reverent acts by human beings, deities, and spirits alike.

For example, a simple devotional ritual to the element of earth could begin by lighting a candle. Take a moment to focus on the flame, then take a deep breath, and shift your focus to the ground beneath your feet. Allow yourself to become aware of how your body feels and, when you are ready, evoke the element of earth by speaking some words out loud. You can experiment with this evocation that I wrote:

> By stone and soil
> Rock and root
> I do evoke the element of earth
> Fecund and green,
> Solid and everlasting
> From your fiery core to your coldest peak,
> Join me here now, as I celebrate your abundance
> I stand on your foundation
> I listen for your wisdom
> I see your beauty

I taste your salt
I smell your perfumes
Be here now and receive my praise

After the earth has been evoked, light the incense. Waft the smoke around your space and bathe yourself in it. Take a moment to be conscious of the presence of earth and note how it makes you feel. Write down your observations in your journal, noting any sensations in your body, temperature changes, or changes in your environment. These can be very subtle, but worth recording. Over time you may notice a pattern, so writing notes each time will help you discover what works for you.

After you have had the time you need to sit with this energy, you should state your intent to release the element of earth and end the devotional ritual:

Element of earth
Thank you for your gracious gifts of abundance
I am grounded by your foundation
I am empowered by your wisdom
I am enraptured by your beauty
I am balanced by your salt
I am enchanted by your perfumes
Thank you for your presence here
Farewell

Extinguish the incense and blow out the candle. Don't forget to make notes in your journal.

Invocation

Invoking an entity and allowing it to possess a human body is a much more involved action, and requires more thought, consideration, and planning. Modern Pagan and Witchcraft traditions that practice true invocation have historically reserved this practice for experienced practitioners and/or dedicated initiates of that particular tradition. With the easy availability of once restricted information on the internet, and in accessible books, a wider audience of interested people are getting the opportunity to learn about these practices, and they are experimenting without the advantage of experienced mentors to learn from. The best advice if you choose to experiment is to take it slow and try to make sure that you have someone working with you as a helper to ensure that if something gets intense, you have support. The experience of being possessed by an entity can be disorienting to the point of being frightening if you are not prepared for it.

Entities can be invoked into their human vessel in various levels. It may take the form of a light trance-like state, in which the vessel is completely aware that the entity is present, right up to a full-on ecstatic possession where the vessel has absolutely no awareness or memory of what happened during the possession at all.

When an entity enters a human body, it can enjoy the sensual pleasures of our world. It may use the body to indulge in food and drink or to dance and experiment with the feeling of being corporeal. This is another good reason to have a helper to watch over the vessel. Entities are not always mindful of the physical danger they may put their mortal vessel in while they are experimenting with their bodies. Getting too close to a candle flame or flight of stairs can lead to serious injury for the vessel.

So how can you tell the difference between a genuine invocation and delusion? There are symptoms that can be felt by the vessel and witnessed by other observers in the room. Therefore, it is wise for the person acting as the vessel to have a helper with them, to watch them for signs that the invocation is taking and note any symptoms that the vessel is displaying. It is important that the helper be familiar with the normal behavior of the vessel, so that they can accurately assess their state. The helper should make note of their observations for future reference.

If the invocation is working, the vessel may:

- close their eyes
- physically relax
- feel pressure or physical discomfort
- experience blurred or tunnel vision
- lose concept of time
- experience emotional outbursts such as inappropriate anger or laughter
- become physically stronger and more agile than normal
- experience amnesia

The helper may observe in the vessel:

- a distinct change in posture or mannerisms
- a change in the condition of the skin such as flushing, sudden paleness, sweating
- a change in vocal pattern such as speaking another language, with a foreign accent or slurred speech
- they no longer require their glasses/hearing aid/cane
- their eyes may not track together
- a change in facial characteristics, unusual eye fluttering, or tics

If the invocation is light, the vessel may feel compelled to say and do things as if prompted by an external power. At this level the presence of the entity is just enough to gently guide and inspire the vessel. At this level the vessel is still in charge of themselves but may subtly alternate control with the entity.

At the next level of invocation, the vessel becomes a more open channel for the entity, but still retains control. This is when the vessel may feel that they are speaking words without knowing where they are coming from, or having insights that they would not ordinarily have. The vessel will more readily surrender to the entity for longer periods of time.

Receiving the invocation at the next deeper level, the vessel may now start to readily display symptoms of possession setting in. They are still in control of themselves and aware of who and where they are, but time may start to become abstract. They may start to display unusual physical behaviors and possibly speak and/or act differently.

And finally, the vessel may undergo complete possession. This is the level where the vessel has surrendered their body to the incoming entity. Now the entity is in charge and can enjoy an earthly body. This is when the aid of the helper is most essential and it is their responsibility to ensure the safety of the vessel and the other participants in the ritual.

After the entity has been released from the vessel, there will be some aftercare required. It is normal for the vessel to need some time to readjust themselves to the mundane world and to look after some basic bodily requirements. In my own coven's practice, when someone returns from being a vessel, the priestess or priest in charge will look the vessel in the eyes, call them by their name, and ask them two questions:

1. "[Insert name here], are you fully present?" The answer should be a clear yes.

2. "Do you have any reason to deceive me?" The answer should be a clear no.

If they are not able to properly answer these questions the helper should address them by their name and ask them to repeat it back to them. The helper can also ask other basic questions, such as what day of the week it is, do they know where they are, etc. The vessel may be tired, hungry, and in need of a bathroom break. Have some food and something non-alcoholic on hand to give them. The helper can offer to escort them to the bathroom and suggest that they splash some water on their face or move their bodies in a familiar and comfortable way.

For some people invocation does not work. This can happen because more practice or training is required, because of distractions or stress not allowing for an appropriate state of mind, or because the practitioner does not sincerely believe that it is possible. This process does imply that you hold a belief that, at some level, these entities are real and capable of actually manifesting and communicating with us. Take a moment to reflect on how you perceive deity, elements, and spirits. How can invoking their presence be a meaningful experience for you? Does belief in a deity, spirit, or element resonate with you? Make a note of this in your journal. Check in with this question periodically to see if your answer changes over time as you have more experience evoking and invoking entities.

I was once asked by a dear friend to act as a vessel for the goddess Isis in a public ritual that was being held at a large hotel-based Pagan conference. As it was scheduled for the evening, against some other fantastic programming, we did not anticipate much of a crowd. We hoped that at least a couple dozen folks would show up. Much to our shock and amazement we got somewhere around sixty attendees, at least. The ritual was based on *The Sea Priestess*, a book of occult fiction by Dion Fortune. Despite being fiction, the book has some beautiful ritual themes and poetry in it. It was our intention to introduce people to the work of the author, explain the context for the stories, and present an interpretation of how the rituals Fortune wrote about could work in real life. Going in, I did not foresee the invocation of Isis to "take," as this was a public ritual, and we had only a limited amount of time together to prepare and rehearse.

The first part of the ritual went as planned. We had to work off scripts to keep us on track as the ritual included a lot of long readings from Dion Fortune's work. Then my friend read the invocation to Isis. He did a great job. I remember feeling slightly nauseated, light-headed, and somewhat intoxicated at this point. I made the conscious decision to let Isis in, surrender to the moment, and let her use my body.

During the next part of the ritual "Isis" was supposed to walk around the circle, pausing at each person, so that they could lift her veil and look into the face of the goddess. I have a memory of being led to the edge of the circle by a priestess assigned to be my helper. I recall seeing the first couple of participants, one of whom is a member of my coven. Then things get very foggy. I have disjointed memories of curious, peering eyes, and of not knowing where my feet were. My coven-mate said she knew I had slipped away when my posture and the way I walk changed.

I snapped back fast when Isis finished her walk around the circle. I knew I needed to be fully present for the next stage of the ritual, and I was. When the ritual was over, I went to the hotel bar and voraciously tore into a steak and a huge glass of wine. Being a vessel is hungry work. I slept like a log that night and woke up feeling quite refreshed.

Making an Offering

It is customary to offer the deities something when you call on them. This may be a show of respect, reverence, or thanks for their gifts when a magical working is successful. It is important to do some research and make sure that the offering you are making is appropriate and will be appreciated. For most deities there is a story describing them and their adventures. Within these stories are clues about the preferences of that deity and details about their personalities. Deities also originate from cultures and geographic regions that can influence what you may choose as an appropriate offering.

When offering food or drink, how much you offer is up to you and what you deem as practical. If you are toasting a deity, pouring a few drops of the beverage on the ground or into a bowl to honour the deity before you drink would suffice. If you are asking the deity for a big boon or favour, pouring out a whole bottle of wine or laying out an adult-sized portion of food may feel more appropriate. Give some serious thought and research into the deity you are appealing to and make your selections as appropriate as possible.

Food: Select food items that are noted in the stories of the deities if possible. If you have a garden, select ripe and beautiful fruits and vegetables that you have tended, and harvest them with intent. Be mindful of the quality of the food you choose. If it is not fit for you to eat, it is not fit for the deities either. This is not an opportunity to clear moldy leftovers out of your fridge; this is the preparation of a sacred offering, so the food you select should be fit for your most honoured guests. Food offerings can be arranged on a plate or pentacle and left on the altar. The plate can be taken outside and left for the deities to take, usually in the form of local wildlife, so please make sure the food is not harmful or toxic to the creatures that may take it. For example, dark chocolate may seem like a great idea, but if you leave it under a tree in your backyard and your dog finds it, it could kill them!

Alcohol: Beer, wine, cider, spirits, or mead can all be used, and certain deities may have a preference. Dionysus may really appreciate a nice bottle of Greek wine, Ogun would enjoy some fine rum, and Ninkasi would like a beer. Open a fresh bottle of carbonated drinks or wine, avoiding flat or stale old bottles from the back of your liquor cabinet. Spirits like rum or whiskey can be previously opened as they keep well. Remember—if it's not good enough for you to enjoy, then why would you serve it to a god? Alcohol may be poured in offering directly onto the earth, over an outdoor shrine, or into a river or stream. If you are making an offering to a forest deity, pour it on the base of a tree. Make the offering as relevant as possible. If your ritual is indoors you can pour it into a cup or bowl and then transfer it outside when possible, or pour it into a plant pot filled with earth.

Incense: The fragrant smoke of incense is a classic offering to deities and spirits in many cultures. The burning of incense is considered a sacrificial offering. The aroma can be experienced and enjoyed by the deities or spirits it is intended for, and also by the practitioner offering it. Many deities have a particular incense associated with them and burning it helps to draw their attention to your work.

Offering your time: It is truly a gift of devotion and reverence to give something of yourself. In our modern world, time is precious and there are so many charities that need help. Study the story of the deity you want to honour and think about what they represent. Volunteering your time to help a homeless shelter in honour of Hestia or working for an environmental advocacy group in honour of Gaia are generous offerings to these deities and can be fulfilling and enriching for you as well.

You may also devote your time to developing a practical skill in honour of your deity, and then share those skills with your community as an extra way of expressing your thanks. Isis is a goddess associated with healing. Taking a first aid course and becoming a certified first responder in her name would be a fitting tribute. You could then volunteer as a first aid provider at events in your community.

Honouring Earth Gods—Building a Shrine

One of the great things about Witchcraft and Pagan practices is that we are all empowered and able to create our own sacred spaces and tributes to the gods and spirits. These can be anything from a small altar set up on the corner of a table to raising standing stones in your back yard. How you do it is only limited by your imagination … and occasionally by building codes.

If you are like me, you probably come home from walks with pockets filled with interesting things you find—shiny stones, bits of sea glass, a pinecone, or maybe a feather or weird bendy twig. I can't resist dried seed pods, or a piece of eggshell fallen from a nest. What do you do with all this stuff? You probably collected these items because in some way they spoke to you, and picking them up to hold and examine them gave you a sense of wonder or satisfaction. All of these found objects can be incorporated into an earth shrine in your home and used as a focal point for devotional or magical work.

To connect with the earth, its deities, and spirits, building a small personal shrine in your home is a practical way to incorporate the aspects of earth that are meaningful to you and your practice. I have one on my desk at home that is simply a small green offering dish filled halfway up with pickling salt. It is only 4.5 inches in diameter, so it doesn't hold much, and I often change out the items decorating it. Sometime the items are seasonal—like an acorn from my backyard and a deep orange carnelian in the autumn, or a pinecone and a polished piece of green aventurine at Yule. As I write this, my little desk shrine is inhabited by an egg-shaped pale blue fluorite and a small figurine of a gnome, originally from a box of Red Rose Tea. The bed of salt they sit on has the added benefit of energetically purifying the air around my workspace. I try to remember to dispose of the salt at least once per moon phase and replace it with fresh salt. Occasionally I may add a pinch of herbs or a few drops of an essential oil, if specific magic is needed.

It is best to use a dish made of something fireproof, in case you choose to add a votive candle to your little shrine. An inexpensive option is one of those terracotta plant pot saucers. They are very earthy in appearance, made from clay, and easy to find.

Here is a suggestion for making one of your own.

INGREDIENTS
> a terracotta saucer from a plant pot (6 to 9 inches in diameter works well)
>
> enough soil, sand, or salt to fill the saucer halfway up
>
> a votive sized candle in an earthy colour
>
> an image or figurine that represents nature to you
>
> any combination of stones, crystals, pebbles, pretty bits of bark, twigs, pinecones, seeds, or any other little found object of natural material that speaks to you

Assemble your shrine according to your own personal taste. It should be as beautiful or as quirky as you want it to be. If you are using a paper image of something that represents nature to you,

you can put it in a small frame and prop it up behind your saucer, or tape it to the wall. If you are including a candle, leave enough room around it so that it doesn't burn your other items. If you share your home with companion animals, make sure that anything you add to your shrine is not toxic to them. Pets can become extremely ill from consuming salt, so use sand or dirt if you can't keep a salt dish out of your pet's reach.

To use your shrine, take a few moments per day to slow down. Light your candle and clear your mind. You may choose to include a prayer to the nature deity you feel closest to, or it may suit you best to spend your time in quiet meditation, focusing on the natural world around you.

Chapter 4

SACRED EARTH SITES

Most individuals who follow earth-based religious or spiritual practices can agree that Earth as a whole is a sacred place, and trying to select specific sites to list is a daunting task. A list of sacred stone circles in Ireland alone, for example, would be 187 items long. It is estimated that virtually every major religion in the world has a sacred mountain associated with it. Add to these the number of groves, grottoes, valleys, and other earthy locations and you can really appreciate the emphasis humans have placed on venerating sacred sites. With that in mind, this chapter will take a look at types of places that specifically embody the earth element, along with some notable examples. We will also look at how some specific stones have become places of pilgrimage and folklore.

To declare a place sacred is very much up to the individual or culture that holds it in that light. It may be because the place possesses exceptional beauty, or that it is linked with something culturally significant. It may even be because of the chemistry between the land and the people who live on it. Some sacred sites are naturally occurring, and some have been either entirely constructed or at least embellished by human hands.

The United Nations Educational, Scientific, and Cultural Organization (UNESCO) works to protect and preserve places that are designated world heritage sites for either cultural or natural reasons. In order to be designated a World Heritage Site, an application must be made proving that the site has "outstanding universal value" under the Convention Concerning the Protection of the World Cultural and Natural Heritage. Applications can be made under three categories: cultural, natural, and a newer category for mixed sites. A cultural site would include man-made structures, monuments, archeological sites, or represent something outstanding to a cultural tradition or civilization, current or historic. A natural site would be a place containing extraordinary beauty, rare flora and fauna, or an important example of the evolution of life on Earth and its geology. The third category can be a site that combines nature and culture. Once a site receives this designation it is protected under the Geneva Convention and can expect to see an elevation in its popularity, which brings tourists. Most importantly, the site can access funding to preserve and protect it.

Some of the most outstanding, beautiful, and spiritual locations on earth are counted among the more than 1,100 places included on UNESCO's list: Machu Picchu in Peru, the Taj Mahal in India, Angkor Wat in Cambodia, Mesa Verde in the United States, the Acropolis of Athens in Greece, and the Pyramids of Giza in Egypt are just a few of the profoundly beautiful and globally significant protected places.

An application from a committee representing Pimachiowin Aki, a large swath of pristine boreal forest in the middle of Canada, challenged UNESCO's understanding of the connection between culture and landscape. Pimachiowin Aki translates to "The Land That Gives Life," and it is the home of four First Nations communities. The Anishinaabeg people of these communities have ancestral connections to this land that reach back for at least seven thousand years. This includes a profound cultural tradition of stewardship that is based on honouring the gifts of the Creator, respect for all life, and living in harmony with others. At the time of the application, UNESCO did not consider the nuances of such an interconnected relationship between culture and nature. This application maintained that from the worldview of the Anishinaabeg people who live there, there is no separation between the two, and that the land and people are one. This unique situation forced UNESCO to re-evaluate its criteria and deepen its understanding of the connection between Indigenous people and the land they see as sacred. Pimachiowin Aki was finally granted World Heritage status in 2018, becoming the largest "mixed" cultural and natural site in North America.

Types of Sacred Earth Sites

In moments when you feel like you need to reconnect to the earth, visiting a sacred place can provide a much-needed opportunity to ground yourself, and recharge your batteries. A walk in the forest to sit under a tree and just breathe the air can soothe jangled nerves, and strolling through a garden, stopping to smell the roses, can give you the perspective you need to get through a stressful day. These may sound like corny or simplistic solutions, but they work. Earth magic does not need to be complicated to be effective.

Caves: These earthy chambers may be naturally occurring or created by humans. For many cultures who view Mother Earth as sacred, a cave is often seen as a womb and used as a place of birth, shelter, protection, and renewal. Because a cave can also be a dangerous place, prone to rockslides, lack of oxygen, and complete darkness, it can also be viewed as a place connected to death and the underworld. The importance of caves in religion and culture is found around the world. The Dikteon Cave, on the island of Crete, is said to be where the goddess Rhea gave birth to the god Zeus. The Actun Tunichil Muknal cave in Belize is accessed by an underworld journey that involves walking, wading and underwater swimming to gain entry. The ancient Maya people used this sacred cave for the ritual sacrifice of human victims. The Elephanta Caves in India are a UNESCO World Heritage site and feature rock art dedicated to the Hindu god Shiva. These man-made caves were constructed in the fifth and sixth centuries CE.

Canyons: These earth features are deep, narrow, and V-shaped valleys, cut into the rock by the movement of a river, erosion, weathering, or tectonic activity. The steep walls reveal layers of the earth's history as the canyon's shape provides a natural cross-cut through the layers of rock around it and access to fossils and evidence of prehistoric life. Smaller versions of canyons are referred to as gorges. Antelope Canyon in Arizona, USA, is located on the land of the LeChee Chapter of the Navajo Nation. It is considered a deeply spiritual and sacred place; it is seen as a symbol of Mother Nature's gifts and it is a place to visit in order to appreciate the passage of time and to be humbled by something that is greater than the self. In South Australia, in Flinders Ranges National Park, is Sacred Canyon, where the Adnyamathanha people decorated the canyon walls with *Yura Marlka* (an artistic form of painting, engraving, and drawing) forty thousand years ago.

Sacred Forests and Groves: Forests and groves have been associated with magic, spirituality, religion, and superstition for as long as humans have been on earth. Some of these places are specifically designated as sacred, and have codes or taboos that must be observed in order to appropriately respect the place and the entities that live there. Access may be limited; hunting or gathering food or wood may be prohibited but, in some places, the taking of specific resources, such as plant medicine or fallen fruit may be allowed. Some are considered sacred because they are believed to be the home of spirits, ghosts, deities, or supernatural creatures. One huge benefit of a forest being officially designated sacred is that it is allowed to remain intact, untouched by the logging industry. This allows the original, native forest species to continue, to preserve an example of the local biodiversity. India is a country with a strong tradition of maintaining sacred forests and groves, and they have more than one hundred thousand of them, in various sizes. They are maintained to provide erosion control and protect water quality, as well as for religious purposes and as a sacred place to bury the dead. Rare and endangered flora and fauna take refuge in India's sacred woodlands as they do in other such designated areas around the world. In China, people in rural areas have been protecting and maintaining "fengshui forests" for centuries. These places were preserved despite the constant, relentless demand for land to convert for agriculture and industrial purposes in order to create harmony with the land and encourage the flow of qi (chi) in and around the community.

Gardens: For anyone who has ever tended a garden, be it a flower garden, vegetable garden, or a well-intended but scruffy patch of good intentions and weeds, there is no doubt that the act of getting your hands dirty and smelling the clean earth is a deeply satisfying and spiritual practice. Food you have grown yourself just tastes better and it is so satisfying to watch a seed you have planted grow to be a beautiful plant. Spending time in the beauty of a garden has the power to heal and reduce stress, and in recognition of this, many hospitals and health care facilities are investing in creating healing gardens to help patients recover from their illnesses. Gardens have the power to bring people together and teach about culture. At the University of Toronto, in Canada, a garden of Indigenous plant medicine was established to provide a gathering place for Indigenous and non-Indigenous people to learn about traditional ceremonies and medicine. Some gardens are created on pre-existing sacred sites, to enhance their inherent qualities and give pilgrims a place to meditate and reflect. The Chalice Well Gardens in Glastonbury, UK, sits in the vale between the gentle Chalice Hill and the iconic Glastonbury Tor. The garden features different zones that gently offer different themes highlighted by the plant choices and views from each space. The focal point of the gardens is the Red Spring, a constant source of iron-rich waters bubbling up from the earth at a consistent rate and temperature and flowing through a series of pools that can be experienced in different ways. The water itself is very earthy and metallic tasting and the iron content leaves behind a rusty red patina wherever it flows.

Ley Lines: These are lines of earth energy that crisscross the planet. The theory that describes them was put forth by Alfred Watkins in 1921, after he noticed a distinct pattern in the countryside he was examining. He realized that the notable ancient points of interest on the land all lined up with one another, across hilltops and great distances, with straight trackways connecting them. Watkins' theory describes how people as far back as the Neolithic era could have used basic surveying methods to plot out these energetic lines, which usually had a distinctive looking hilltop as at least one of their terminal points. Along the trackways, markers were placed to help travelers navigate. The markers that Watkins found were trees, cairns (typical of upland settings), mark stones (in lowland settings), ponds, ditches or pools of water, actual roads, or mounds. Some of these markers seem to have inspired communities to grow up around them or have actual roads built on their foundation. The presence of churches on ley lines supports a theory that they were built on pre-Christian sacred sites that were part of the ley line trackway system. These significant points on the ley lines are thought to be where earth energy is more concentrated and available to be used for spiritual or occult purposes. The layers of development along ley lines indicates that there was a working knowledge and tradition of them over many centuries that grew and developed over time before being slowly forgotten. In the modern age, many of the places that the trackways would have been were dug up, paved, and developed to make way for our present civilization, leaving only fragments for us to try to understand. The most extensive research on ley lines has been carried out in Great Britain, but they have been discovered to a lesser extent around the world.

Mountains and Hills: The concept of climbing a mountain to reach enlightenment or become closer to deity is cross-cultural. The silhouette of a mountain or a hill on a landscape creates an icon that the communities around it claim as part of their cultural identity. In Maori culture, mountains are regarded as ancestors, and possess Mana, or spiritual power. To climb a mountain and stand on its peak is an insult, it is as if you are standing on the head of a beloved ancestor.

On the top of the highest mountain in Greece, Mount Olympus, was the home of the twelve principal deities in the Greek pantheon. The steepest peak of the mountain, Stefani, is said to be the throne of Zeus, and the highest peak, Mytikas, was the site where the Olympian gods would gather. Mount Sinai in Egypt is regarded as sacred by the Jewish, Muslim, and Christian faiths, as this is where it is believed that Moses received the Ten Commandments from God.

The Black Hills are a small range of mountains that run from South Dakota into Wyoming and Montana in the United States. This is the traditional territory of the Lakota Sioux and is sacred. It is referred to as Paha Sapa, "the heart of everything that is." Treaties between the Indigenous people and the white settlers were struck in 1851 and again in 1868, but both were broken. The latter fell apart when gold was discovered, and the resulting gold rush brought miners and more settlers and war. The battle for the land continues in court, with the surviving Lakota Sioux refusing to take money for the land that they refuse to sell. The additional insult of Mount Rushmore, a monument celebrating European settlers who appropriated unceded Sioux land, stands as a questionable memorial that for many people represents white supremacy and the need for reconciliation.

Petroforms: In North America, Indigenous people used rocks and boulders of various sizes to create mosaics or pictures on the ground, usually in flat, open areas. These stones are placed on the ground and not piled on top of each other, which makes them vulnerable to being displaced by natural forces, animals, or careless humans. Because they are lying on the surface with no telltale soil or deposits covering them, it is difficult to date how old the picture is. The original intent of these creations is unclear, but the ones remaining today are considered deeply sacred, and some are still used as places for ceremony, healing, teaching, and gathering. The Bannock Point Petroforms, located in the Whiteshell Provincial Park, Manitoba, Canada, are a remarkable example. The stones are laid out in the shapes of humans, turtles, snakes, geometric patterns, and a thunderbird. They are believed to be prehistoric, but the exact age, purpose, and who placed them on the expansive smooth rock ground is a mystery.

Megaliths: By far some of the most iconic and world-famous sacred earth sites involve some form of megalith. These are simply large stones that are set either alone, or with other stones, into the landscape for practical or ceremonial purposes. There are tens of thousands of megaliths around the world, but the largest concentration of them can be found in Great Britain, Ireland, France, and Brittany. They were most commonly erected during the Neolithic period, during a time when humans were settling down, building permanent communities, and developing agriculture. There are several terms to describe the various types of megaliths:

- A **cairn** is a man-made pile of stones used to mark a significant site, such as a trail or burial, or for ceremonial purposes.
- A **menhir** is a tall, vertical standing stone. They are shaped by humans and can appear individually or in groups. The remains of the largest known menhir can be found at Locmariaquer, France. It was erected around 4700 BCE and would have stood more than twenty meters tall and weighed 280 tonnes. It is unknown how exactly this massive stone was hoisted into place, or why. It fell and broke within a few hundred years of being put up, and the best guess is that it was due to an earthquake.

- A **dolmen** is a type of stone construction involving at least two upright stones that support a horizontal stone, forming a table-like structure. Some dolmens would have been covered over with soil and turf, creating mounds, and some would have been used as burial chambers. The largest dolmen in Europe is the Brownshill Dolmen, located outside of Carlow, in Ireland. It was built around 4000 BCE and the horizontal capstone weighs 150 tons. The effort and engineering required to move a stone like this without modern machinery is mind-boggling.

The reasons for constructing these megaliths are varied, and many reasons are lost in the mists of time. Some stone circles align with the movements of the sun or moon and appear to be observatories or calendars. Menhirs are reported to be originally intended as memorials or boundary markers.

Megaliths of all types are fascinating to explore. The age and size of the massive stones, and the mystery of how and why they were placed, captures the imagination and invokes wonder. The magnitude of difficulty to transport and then erect a monument of such weight and size with only the muscle of humans and animals to get the job done is a testament to how important it must have been.

The title for the most famous megalith of all can easily be awarded to Stonehenge. Located on the Salisbury Plain in Wiltshire, England, this ancient stone monument was constructed in several stages over at least 1,500 years. Who built Stonehenge and why is a mystery, but the important thing is to appreciate that it has been a sacred site to a variety of people since it was first created, and remains so to this day.

Terrestrial Zodiacs: These are also referred to as landscape zodiacs, and they are thought to be man-made, presumably ancient, giant-scale maps of the heavens. They are created by incorporating natural and artificial features from the landscape, such as roads, waterways, hills, and earthworks, to create a reflection of the stars above. The best-known of these can be found in the countryside in and around the town of Glastonbury, in Somerset, UK. Known as "Glastonbury's Temple of the Stars," a name given to it by the writer Katherine Maltwood, it forms a circle across the landscape that is 16 kilometers (10 miles) across. Through the 1930s, Maltwood was a prolific writer on this zodiac, suggesting that these shapes had been originally created in the prehistoric era, making the most of the natural landscape with some human embellishments. These theories are not widely accepted as true, as some of the features included in this zodiac are too modern. What is true is that the existence of what people believe to be a terrestrial zodiac is inspiring and thought-provoking, and it provides real opportunities for spiritual growth and connection. There are now thought to be more than sixty terrestrial zodiacs across the UK.

Tumulus: These burial mounds are also sometimes called barrows or kurgans. These are piles of earth and/or stone that cover one or more graves; they can be found around the world and usually date back to ancient history. The style of the tumuli (plural form) will vary according to culture. The Newgrange burial mound in County Meath, Ireland, was constructed 5,200 years ago as a tomb, but it also has significant astrological, religious, and ceremonial functions. It is a substantial monument measuring 85 meters (279 feet) in diameter. The passageway leading inside is oriented to align with the rising sun at the winter solstice and it is thought to represent the promise of new life to those who have died.

Significant Stones

Stones have had religious, ceremonial, magical, and spiritual significance for humans since pre-history. The fascination with stones crosses cultures, religions, and time. There is something deep in the human DNA that is attracted to stones and creates a need to connect with them and use them as symbols of the things we hold sacred. Maybe we can feel that they resonate with some trace of home, or a place we long to return to or carry with us. In some instances, the stone is sacred because it was once in contact with a revered figure or is perceived to have supernatural power.

Black Stone of Mecca *(Hajar al-Aswad)*: This sacred Islamic stone has many origin stories including that it was given to Adam when he was banished from Eden, to absorb his sin, and that the stone was originally from heaven. It is not known what kind of stone it is, but it is rumored to be a meteorite, which could explain the lore about it falling from heaven. The stone has a colourful history, having been the target of theft, and damaged by war. As a result, it is broken into several pieces and held together by a silver frame. It is housed in the eastern wall of the Ka'bah, a shrine that is part of the Great Mosque of Mecca, where pilgrims come from around the world to participate in the ritual of the *hajj*. It is expected that at least once in their life, every Muslim will attend this rite in which they walk counterclockwise seven times around the Ka'bah and try to kiss the Black Stone, as it is believed that the prophet Mohammad also kissed it. With more than two million Muslims visiting each year, the Black Stone of Mecca is probably the most venerated stone in history.

Blarney Stone: This legendary stone was set in a tower at Blarney Castle in county Cork, Ireland, in 1446 and has several questionable origin stories. It is made of carboniferous limestone and, as the story goes, will bestow the gift of eloquence on anyone who kisses it. The knowledge of this power was revealed to the king of Munster by an old woman, who turned out to be a witch, as thanks for saving her from drowning. Tens of thousands of people visit every year to climb the tower and kiss the stone.

Inuksuit: The singular form of the word is *inuksuk*, which translates as "to act in the capacity of a human." These stone constructions are built by Inuit people of the Arctic to act as navigational aids, mark out good hunting grounds, convey personal messages, warn travelers of potential hazards, or commemorate the dead. To an untrained eye, many inuksuit appear to be stones and boulders piled on top of each other, sometimes leaning in a particular direction or stacked in such a way as to have a "window" in the middle. To the *Inummariit* ("the people who knew how to survive on the land living in a traditional way"), these are readable signposts carrying vital information. Inuksuit were also erected for spiritual purposes. Some mark spiritual boundaries or areas that need to be left alone, or were sacred places to leave offerings and ask for healing or protection.

Moai of Easter Island: The indigenous name for the island is Rapa Nui and it can be found in the Pacific Ocean 3,540 kilometers (2,200 miles) west of Chile. The moai are massive stone statues that stand up to 10 meters in height and weigh up to 86 tons. There are thought to be as many as one thousand of them on the island. They are carved from a volcanic stone called *tuff*, which is soft enough to carve with stone tools. When the Rapa Nui people created them is unknown, but they appear to have been created in three phases between 400 and 1500 BCE. The looming statues were made to represent the leaders and important people of the island who had died. Once created, they would be "walked" to the *ahus*, using ropes or logs to maneuver them. An ahu is a large platform, sometimes containing a burial chamber, and the maoi would be positioned on top, staring inland. How the islanders moved these giants is up for debate, but the local lore says that the maoi would walk on their own to their resting place.

Omphalos Stone: Omphalos is an ancient Greek word that means "navel." There is more than one reference to such stones in Greek mythology, and many examples of omphalos exist around the world, but the most famous is the one that was found in the ruins of the oracular temple at Delphi. Legend has it that Zeus sent two eagles off in opposite directions and ordered them to meet at the centre of the world. The eagles met again at Delphi, and to mark this spot Zeus laid down a large rounded and slightly pointed white stone, inscribed with carvings to denote that this was the "navel of the world." There is an omphalo stone found in Armenia near the town of Sisian called the Portakar, or navel stone. It is believed that a woman wishing to get pregnant can increase her fertility by lying on top of it and pressing her belly against the stone.

Rosetta Stone: This impressive piece of black granodiorite, weighing 760 kg (1,680 lbs) was once part of a larger stone slab. Written upon it is a decree about the king Ptolemy and it dates from around 196 BCE. The message inscribed on the stone is significant not because of its content, but because it was carved in three languages: ancient Greek, Demotic (the everyday language of the Egyptian people), and in Egyptian hieroglyphs. At the time it was found, nobody knew how to read the hieroglyphs as it had become a dead language. The inclusion of the ancient Greek on the stone meant that the hieroglyphs could be translated and understood. The Rosetta Stone became the key for unlocking the mystery of the ancient Egyptian symbols. It was apparently rediscovered by French soldiers in Napoleon's army in 1799 while they were digging the foundation for a fort near the town of Rashid, Egypt. When Napoleon was defeated, the stone was handed over to the British, who shipped it back to England, where it now resides on permanent display in the British Museum. It is considered one of the most famous pieces in their entire collection.

Stone of Scone: This 152 kg (336 pound) block of sandstone is thought to have travelled through Egypt, Spain, and Sicily before it made its way to Ireland in approximately 700 BCE. It sat on the Hill of Tara and was used in the coronation ceremonies of the kings of Ireland until it was captured by Celtic Scots, who knew it as Lia Fail, "the speaking stone." It was moved to Scotland, finally resting in Scone, where it was used in the coronation ceremonies of their kings. It was captured again in 1296, this time by Edward I of England, who took it to Westminster Abby in London. The stone has remained in use until this day, serving as the seat on which most English rulers have been crowned ever since. It was the target of a conspiracy of four Scottish students who stole the stone on Christmas Day 1950 and took it back to Scotland in order to raise support for the fight for Scottish independence. Unfortunately, the stone was broken in half during the theft. The conspirators split up, and the two halves of the stone were separated. After some harrowing adventures and a media circus, the two halves were reunited, and the stone repaired. It was left at Arbroath Abbey in April 1951 and, once the authorities found out, returned to England. It remained there until 1996, when the British government returned it to Scotland, where it now resides in Edinburgh Castle.

Sword in the Stone, Montesiepi Chapel, Italy: Not to be confused with that other sword in the stone from Arthurian myth, this one is Italy's version of the Excalibur story and it belonged to Galgano Guidotti, a twelfth-century retired knight who became a religious hermit. Guidotti, who had been a selfish and sinful soldier, began having visions of the Archangel Michael. He retreated to a cave, only to be lured out by a request from his family. As he rode past a hill called Montesiepi, he was thrown from his horse and had another vision. The archangel told him to renounce all material things, and Guidotti replied that it would be easier to split a rock. To prove it, he thrust his sword into a rock, and it slid easily into the stone "like butter." The stone with the sword still in it is on display at the Montesiepi Chapel to this day. Many have tried to steal it, and others have tried to debunk it. It was examined by scientists in 2001, who confirmed that it is at least old enough to have belonged to someone living in Guidotti's time.

Significant Trees

Human beings have a profound relationship with trees. We are inherently drawn to these slow, strong, and silent witnesses to time and history. Trees speak to us on a subliminal level. They stand silently breathing alongside us; they inspire art and poetry; and they provide us with fuel, shelter, and a wide array of products and comforts. We seek the solace and contemplation of a walk in the woods or the relief of their shade, but how often do we make an effort to provide anything for the trees?

Different religions and cultures have designated entire species of trees as sacred. The baobab tree, which grows in parts of Africa, is revered for its ability to provide food, shelter, and water. They grow to an immense size, up to 30 meters (98 feet) tall, and can live for five thousand years. Throughout history, the olive tree has been considered sacred by the Greeks. Its fruits are eaten or pressed for their valuable oil and used in a multitude of applications. An olive branch is a universal symbol of peace.

Individual trees that have extraordinary age or size become places of pilgrimage; some of them become so famous that they have larger-than-life "personalities." We plan vacations to visit them, decorate and leave offerings to them, name them, and feel connected to them. Special trees become landmarks and signposts for our travels and for our lives.

Bodhi Tree *(India)*: Located in Bodh Gaya in Bihar, India, is a living descendant of the original fig tree (*Ficus religiosa*), referred to as the Bodhi Tree, that Buddha sat beneath and meditated until he reached enlightenment. This site is a significant place of pilgrimage for Buddhists from around the world and is considered to be among the religion's most sacred locations. December 8 is celebrated as Bodhi Day in honour of Buddha's time under the tree and the birth of Buddhism.

Brian Boru Oak *(Ireland)*: This majestic oak is thought to be about one thousand years old; it is named for Brian Boru, the last high king of Ireland, who was also born in the area. Located near the village of Tuamgraney in County Clare, this oak is part of the Raheen Woods, and is a rare specimen of the type of oak trees that once covered Ireland. The island was once heavily forested, with at least 75 percent of the land taken up with rich forests. Now only 10 percent of the country has forest, and less than 1 percent of that is native woodland. The Brian Boru Oak draws visitors who want to touch history and imagine what this mighty forest once looked like.

Methuselah Date Palm *(Israel)*: In 1963, six seeds from a now-extinct subspecies of date palm were discovered on an excavation of the Masada fortress in Israel. They were later radiocarbon dated and it was confirmed that they were very old indeed, from somewhere between 155 BCE and 64 CE. It wasn't until 2005 that the decision was made to try planting some of the seeds. Three were selected and miraculously, one sprouted and flourished. The tree is now more than ten feet tall and has successfully pollinated with a modern date palm and produced fruit, allowing modern scientists to actually have a taste of history. Since this success, six more ancient date palm seeds found in the region have been successfully sprouted; they will assist with research into the medicinal and nutritional properties of these trees. Named after the biblical figure who lived to be more than nine hundred years old, Methuselah the tree is growing at Kibbutz Ketura in Israel.

Giant Sequoias *(United States)*: These magnificent trees grow to be among the largest trees on the planet. They can reach a diameter of 9 meters (30 feet) and a height of 76 meters (250 feet). The oldest recorded sequoia lived for more than 3,500 years. They were once found scattered across the Northern Hemisphere, but now their domain is reduced to a humble collection of seventy-seven groves in Northern California. Every year, thousands of tourists flock to see the towering giants at national parks, for a photo op and a chance to commune with these awesome beings.

When these preserves were established, some of the sequoias were given names to commemorate civil war heroes, which may have seemed like a good idea at the time. At least three of these gentle giants had been named for General Robert E. Lee, a slave-holder and Confederate leader. In the summer of 2020, in light of the movement to remove statues and monuments that pay tribute to slaveholders and racists, park officials made the decision to remove all signage and references to the Lee name on these trees. The trees can only be officially renamed by Congress or the National Parks Director, but at the park level, it was deemed no longer appropriate for the names to stand, and against the best intentions of the park to be a welcoming and inclusive place for all people to enjoy nature.

The Holy Thorn *(England)*: Standing on the windswept Wearyall Hill, overlooking the town of Glastonbury in Somerset County, the Holy Thorn is a destination for devout Christians and curious tourists from every spiritual path. According to legend, after the crucifixion of Jesus Christ, his uncle, Joseph of Arimathea, travelled on a trading voyage to England. Upon arriving, he and his twelve companions climbed the hill to look around. He stuck his staff in the ground while he and his party rested. When they awoke the next day, his staff had miraculously taken root. The Holy Thorn continued to grow and flower, and not just in the spring as expected, but also at Christmas. In the seventeenth century the thorn trees (there were said to be three of them by this time) were cut down by Puritan soldiers. Legend has it that local people saved cuttings and kept the Holy Thorn alive by nurturing them. The Holy Thorn that stands on the hill today is said to be descended from those cuttings, and it has been the target of serious vandalism in recent years.

PART
2

WORKING WITH THE ELEMENT OF EARTH

Chapter 5

THE ELEMENT OF EARTH IN MAGIC

The element of earth brings definition, form, and matter to magic. It possesses the qualities of endurance, commitment, wisdom, and practicality. Earth takes time; it moves slowly and steadily. Earth documents and keeps records and layers knowledge with experience. Earth is creative and fertile; it manifests and produces. Earth knows when to be silent, when to make its move, and when to speak. Earth is calm and dependable, providing the foundation and routine for our rituals and our practice.

Getting Grounded and Centred

One of the very first things taught to new practitioners of magic and ritual is how to "ground and centre" themselves. It is a practice commonly used at the beginning of a ritual or ceremony in order to get into a calm and focused state of mind. This is your opportunity to clear your mind of all the mundane chatter from your day and park any concerns or anxiety you may be carrying outside of your sacred space, freeing your mind up to do your magical work.

The Tree of Life

The purpose of grounding is to connect yourself energetically to the earth. There are myriad ways to do this; many of them include some kind of guided visualization. Popular ones often involve "Tree of Life" imagery, or something similar. Here is a very simple technique you can try to get you started.

The first step is to set your intention and consciously make the decision to become grounded. Next, check in with your physical body and be aware of your posture. If you are sitting, as much as possible, make sure your feet are planted on the ground and your back is straight with your head up. If you are standing, position your feet shoulder-width apart with your hands by your sides. I find it very helpful to stretch and then shake out my arms and legs before I ground. It gives me a chance to check in with how my body feels, and gets my blood moving just enough to be aware of it.

The second step is to check in with your breathing. Start by taking a slow deep breath, inhaling as deeply and deliberately as you can. Hold it for a moment, and then slowly exhale. Do this at least three times, or until you feel your mind start to settle down and focus only on your breath.

On your next exhale, visualize that you are shooting roots down out of the bottom of your feet. When you inhale, reflect on the rooted feeling. Exhale and let the roots go deeper. Inhale, reflect. Do this several times, until you feel that the roots are supporting you and your connection to the earth is secure.

Once you feel that you are comfortably grounded, the next step is to centre. The purpose of centring is to become fully aware and connected to yourself. Doing this may take some experimentation at first because you need to find that spot in your body that you associate with the centre of your true self. I find this in the area of my heart and solar plexus, and this is pretty common. Some people may find this is their throat or head, and this will work the same way.

Focus on the roots that you have established by grounding. Then visualize the earth's energy moving up your roots, through your feet, legs, and hips into your centre. Feel the vitality and energizing support that the earth has to offer and breathe through it. Take a moment to experience this, and then allow it to continue upward through your shoulders, arms, neck, and out through the crown of your head. Now, instead of roots, this energy is branches, reaching up to the sky. You are now connected above and below, standing at centre.

With a bit of practice, you will be able to go through this process as quickly or as slowly as you need to. Being properly grounded and centred, you will be able to work magic more effectively and be fully present for the experience. It is also very beneficial to use the same technique any time you feel stressed or unable to focus. Finding a way to ground and centre yourself is a basic magical skill and mundane coping mechanism.

Grounding Together

If you are working with a group, there is one more step that you can take together to gel the combined energy of the participants. After the group has individually grounded and centred, take a moment to consciously connect to the other people you are working with. This can be as simple as deliberately making eye contact with each person as you join hands and form a circle. You may also designate one person to lead a simple guided meditation in which you all visualize your roots and then branches wrapping around each other. When my coven meets, we like to start our rituals by standing together in a circle and then chanting three long tones. The first tone is our grounding tone, the second is our centring tone. With the third tone, we extend our awareness to the group and combine our energies for the ritual to come. Because we do this every time we gather, we have become quite adept at it, and it also has the effect of changing our consciousness, clearing away the outside world, and getting everyone into a circle frame of mind.

Four-Fold Breath

Some of the best training I ever received in how to ground myself came to me through the yoga classes I have taken over the years. In yoga, the practice of breath control is called pranayama. By having a conscious awareness of the breath, the body of the practitioner becomes relaxed yet energized and the mind enters a state conducive to meditation.

An effective and relatively simple technique for grounding yourself is a breathing technique known as *sama vritti pranayama* in my yoga class or, as it later became known to me through my Witchcraft studies, the Four-Fold Breath. One of my Witchcraft teachers picked up this technique from a mentor and was taught this as part of their training in the Golden Dawn system. I have since learned that this way of breathing is also referred to as box breathing, and it is used by US Navy Seals as a way to stay calm and avoid panic in tense situations. It has become such a popular and widespread technique because it works and is simple to do.

When our bodies are under stress, agitated, or in a panic state, we tend to breathe fast and shallowly, and it causes the heart to pound. You can gain control over this and ground yourself by intentionally taking control of your breathing and focusing your anxious or busy mind on counting to four at each of the four stages of the breath.

Start by finding a comfortable sitting position. Adjust yourself so that you may sit this way comfortably without needing to shift or change position for at least five minutes. Make sure that your spine is as straight as possible, and that you can close your eyes and not be disturbed.

Next, pay attention to your own breathing. Inhale and exhale normally for a few breaths and try to just focus on the sensation of the air as it is drawn into, and then expelled from, your lungs.

When you are ready, focus on inhaling and count to four.

Hold your breath for a count of four.

Exhale evenly for a count of four.

Pause, with your lungs empty, for a count of four.

Do not force or strain yourself. If a count of four feels too long at first, try a count of two or three, and work up to four. How slowly or quickly you count will be up to you. Start by doing this whole cycle at least four times and work up to being able to sit comfortably and maintain the Four-Fold Breath for several minutes. You will know you are grounded when a sense of focus and calm comes over you.

Creating an Earth Altar

Creating an altar for doing earth magic can help you connect more deeply to the element. By building a space that features the sensory experiences of earth, you can immerse yourself in the element and commune with it whenever you need or want to. This is a physical focal point of your magical practice. It provides the stage on which to set your tools, symbols, and energy for a magical working. This is a workspace, a place to do divination, meditate, work spells, and pay tribute to the element of earth.

I have two earth altars inside my home. One is on a small shelf above my desk in my office. It has a small statue of an earth goddess type figure, a dish of salt, several natural rocks and tumbled stones, an incense burner, a deck of tarot cards, and a green candle. For my day job in film, and for my writing, I often work from home. I maintain this altar and use it to perform any magical work I may need to assist me with my work. Career, finances, material stability, and security are all related to the attributes of the earth element, so it is fitting to have the earth element honoured and accessible here.

The other earth altar I have set up is in the room I am fortunate enough to have solely dedicated as a temple space. This altar consists of a wooden table that has been in my family for generations, decorated with a large green candle, an antler, and a carved wooden pentacle. It is centred on the north wall of the temple room and the art on the wall above it features photographs I took of Stonehenge, images of the Green Man, and a green and brown colour scheme. All the items and colours chosen for both altars are selected for their association with the element of earth. These things evoke the atmosphere, sensations, and emotions I associate with this element, and enhance the power and experience of working with them.

Start by selecting an area in your home where you want to set your earth altar. This is a working space, after all, so it has to be practical. This altar can be of any size that works for the space. Consider creating a small one near where you do mundane work in your home. Just as I have one in my office where I earn my living, you may want one in your kitchen, where you do your cooking and domestic work. The kitchen is also the equivalent to the hearth of the modern home, and that also fits very nicely with the nature of this element.

Any flat surface can serve as an altar, but it is nice to designate a special table, desk, shelf, or cabinet for the purpose. It is a bonus if the furniture you select has built-in storage for holding extra ritual supplies.

Typically, an altar will be covered with some kind of cloth. Choose a fabric that has a colour association with earth—green, brown, black, or white work well. If your altar is made of wood or another natural material, you may want to use it as-is. As you will no doubt be using candles and other things that can drip, leak, and make a mess, it is a great idea to acquire a piece of tempered glass to protect the altar surface. This is much easier to wipe clean and scrape dripped wax off of if you put it on top of your altar cloth. I have a piece of glass that had been salvaged out of an old refrigerator where it had served as a shelf. It works perfectly and is very durable.

The items you place on your altar are up to your own personal taste and aesthetic. A dish of dirt or salt and a pentacle would be a good start, along with a green or brown candle. Natural beeswax candles smell great and have a rustic, earthy look that suits the element. For incense, pine, cedar, or patchouli are usually pretty easy to find. Print out photos of natural spaces that are significant to you and use those to decorate your altar. Incorporate something that represents your career. For example, if you work as a carpenter, place some nails on your altar, or if you have a business card, add that. Perhaps you have a tool or implement that represents your labour or work to provide the necessities of life for yourself and your family, or a domestic item that has been handed down from an ancestor. I own a potato masher that belonged to my grandmother. It may sound silly, but I have so many early childhood memories of her swearing as she mashed potatoes to make pierogi filling! She made the best perogies, so displaying her masher represents comfort, good food, and a beloved ancestor. An earth connection, albeit an odd one.

I also have a very discreet earth altar outside of my home. At the base of a mountain ash tree in my back yard, I have a large flat rock. This is the place where ritual offerings are left, and libations are poured out. Even if the ritual happened inside the house, a piece of the ritual food and a measure of the ritual wine is left on this stone for the gods when we are done. I am careful to make sure that anything left on the rock is not harmful to the local wildlife, as it is the bunnies and squirrels who seem more than happy to act on behalf of the gods and carry off the bits of oatcake that are most often left there.

Consider the environmental impact of your altar. As Pagans and witches, we are working with the seasons and cycles of nature, so it stands to reason that this reverence should be actively reflected in the choices we make when we are purchasing and selecting ritual items and consumables. Whenever possible, try to select items that are recyclable and biodegradable. Forage mindfully for natural items to bring in from outside. It is the quality of the magic, not the quantity of the "stuff," that matters.

Your altar should be regarded as special and treated with respect. I do not allow it to be used as a place to plop down an empty drink cup or candy wrapper. Any other flat surface can be there for that, but your altar should be a spiritual focal point of your home, and caring for it can be part of your devotional routine.

A few considerations:

- Do keep your altar fresh and tidy. This is a special space where you invite the element of earth, work magic, and attend to your spiritual practice, and it should be maintained in a thoughtful way.

- Do change it up in honour of the seasons, sabbats, and moon phases.
- Do not use it as a place to stack clutter or garbage.
- Do not leave burning candles or incense unattended.
- Do try to the best of your ability to decorate your altar with locally sourced items and tools of natural origin. Items made of wood, stone, metal, natural fabrics, glass, beeswax, etc., have their own vibration to contribute to your magic.
- Do not use plastic and synthetic ritual items whenever possible. These materials are magically inert and do not contribute energetically to your work. From an environmental perspective, they won't biodegrade and will live on in a landfill long after your use for them has ended.

Magical Tool of Earth: The Pentagram

The image of the pentagram is inextricably linked with magic and the occult. There are several symbols and tools that have similar-sounding names but different uses, so let's clear up some confusion and clarify some meanings:

- A *pentagram* is an equilateral five-pointed star shape. It is sometimes referred to as a *pentangle*.
- The word *pentacle* has several meanings. In most modern Pagan and Witchcraft contexts it is described as an equilateral five-pointed star within a circle. A pentacle is also the name for the disk or plate with a five-pointed star carved or drawn on it that often holds food or offerings in a ritual. This may also be used as a focal point on which items are placed to be magically charged during a

working. It often refers to a mystical or magical symbol that does not include the star shape.

- A *paten* is a ceremonial dish that is often made of a precious metal. It is a word that refers to the plate that holds the Eucharist in Christian rituals, but the word does cross over to Pagan ceremonies as well, as the plate that holds offerings or ceremonial food.

The pentagram or pentacle are both symbols used to represent Witchcraft and Wicca in contemporary culture and are prevalent throughout not only magical practices but in mundane ones as well, and they are used in several ways. In some Wiccan traditions, an inverted pentacle or pentagram is used to represent the second degree, and the upright version with the addition of a triangle over the top point is used to indicate the third degree. Early Christians believed that the points on a pentagram represented the wounds of Christ; in Japan it is associated with the five traditional elements of water, wood, earth, fire, and metal, and it also appears on the national flags of Ethiopia and Morocco. The influence and significance of this symbol is universal and powerful. It is important to take the context in which you find it into account before making any assumptions about how it is being used.

Not all pentacles contain pentagrams. Éliphas Lévi wrote about such pentacles as magical symbols in his book *The Key of Solomon the King*. In this text he describes how to make pentacles in detail and describes them as having Hebrew letters, alchemic symbols, six-pointed stars, and geometric shapes. These pentacles are used to control spirits and elements and provide protection from several threats. They can be made of metal or drawn on parchment and have a system of colour and planetary correspondences.

The points on a pentagram each correspond with a different element. The most recognized system for this was developed by a ceremonial magic group called the Hermetic Order of the Golden Dawn toward the end of the nineteenth century. This system has been adopted by many modern Witchcraft, ceremonial magic, and New Age traditions and is the closest thing to a standardized system currently available.

Point up or point down? When used in modern Witchcraft and Wicca, the point on a pentagram or pentacle is usually directed upward. Ceremonial magic groups, such as the Golden Dawn, stated that this was to indicate the element of spirit presiding over the other four elements. The inverted version of the pentagram or pentacle means the opposite—that the earthly elements and desires will overrule spirit. The inverted symbol has become strongly associated with the satanic movement. The inverted pentagram with the added image of a goat's head is called the Sigil of Baphomet.

The Pentagram of Earth

The drawing of a pentagram in the air to evoke or banish a given elemental energy is a procedure that made its way into Pagan and Witchcraft practice via the ceremonial magic stream. This is usually done when casting a circle and calling the elemental quarters, each one having a designated pattern to evoke it at the beginning of the ritual, and then reversing this pattern to banish it at the end of the ritual. In many traditions, the evoking and banishing pentacle of earth is the default pentacle, and it is used at each quarter, so how you do this is up to you. It's a good idea to experiment and find out what you are more drawn to. Once you get the hang of how the pattern is created, it becomes easier to remember.

The purpose of drawing the evoking pentagram is to provide a doorway for the elemental energy to come into the circle and give it focus. To draw an evoking pentacle of earth, you can use the index finger of your dominant hand (if you are right-handed use your right, left-handed use left), or your athame if you have one, in your dominant hand. Stand facing the north and visualize the qualities and attributes of earth. Raise your finger or athame to about shoulder height in front of you. Then draw a deep breath, pulling up energy from the ground beneath your feet and visualize it as a stream of light coursing up through your body and out through your finger or athame. (I see this light as being an electric blue colour; you may see something different.) Use the stream of light to draw your evoking earth pentagram in the air in front of you using this pattern:

The idea is to start drawing at the top of the pentagram, the one ascribed to spirit, and then stroke down to the point of earth and continue in a clockwise pattern until you return to spirit. Some practitioners also like to encircle the pentagram to make it into a pentacle.

The evoking pentacle of earth is a highly effective protective symbol. It may be drawn in the air, or in actuality, to lend protection to a person, place, or thing. To protect or "ward" your home you can draw the earth pentacle using salt water and your finger over each doorway, window, or opening to the dwelling. It is also equally effective to visualize the pentacles being drawn if it is not practical to physically do so.

To banish, you reverse the pattern used to evoke. Starting at the point ascribed to earth and using the index finger of your receptive hand (if you are right-handed use your left, left-handed use right), or your athame if you have one, in your receptive hand, stroke upward to spirit and then continue counterclockwise until you return to spirit. As you do this, visualize the light of the pentagram being sucked back up by your finger or athame, coursing back down through your body and draining back down to the ground where it came from.

The Altar Pentacle

When it appears on an altar as a magical tool, the pentacle can appear as a flat disk or plate inscribed with a pentagram or pentacle shape. It will sometimes have other symbols also inscribed on it, such as elemental or zodiacal symbols, glyphs, sigils, or other symbols sacred to the owner. These can be made of wood, clay, metal, or any number of man-made materials, and they are typically between four and nine inches in diameter—like a tea saucer up to a dinner plate. The size and material choices are really up to the aesthetic that the user prefers, or that their tradition recommends. I would suggest that, as this is a tool of earth, it really should be made of a natural earthy material.

The pentacle is often used as a plate on which food for the ritual participants is placed. In Wiccan-style rituals, the pentacle and the cup are used together for the part of ritual called "cakes and ale" or "cakes and wine." This simple feast is seen as an opportunity to partake in sustenance that has been ritually blessed. It is a metaphor for the divine union and love that creates and sustains all life.

Magical Tool of Earth: Salt

Sodium chloride (NaCl) is the chemical name for salt, and it is one of the most abundant minerals on earth. On average, the oceans and seas of the world are 3.5 percent saline, and all the salt in the world originated from the sea. The deposits of salt found underground that are extracted by mining are the remains of ancient seabeds. For thousands of years, human beings have benefited from being able to save and store precious food using salt as a preservative, and to enjoy the delicious flavours salt adds to the food when eaten. It is essential to human life as it regulates blood pressure and balances the fluids in our bodies. It also ensures that our nerves and muscles work properly. Salt is also an effective healer. Bathing in salt water can soothe sore muscles and treat some skin problems; gargling with salt water can cure sore throats and canker sores.

Salt has such a fundamental significance in our lives that it even influences our language. To call someone the "salt of the earth" is to praise them for being a pure, kind, and honest person. When someone is said to be "worth their salt" it is a comment on how competent and deserving they are of praise or their salary (a word that is from the Latin "sal" meaning salt).

There is a wealth of lore around salt and the various ways it can bring luck, both good and bad. In the painting *The Last Supper* by Leonardo da Vinci, Judas is shown knocking over a cellar of salt with his elbow as Jesus reveals that he knows one of his disciples will betray him. Spilled salt at the dinner table is believed to incite a family argument, and cause trouble not for the spiller, but the person sitting nearest to them.

When I was a kid, my grandmother told me that if you spilled salt it gave the devil an opportunity to get you, and the way to stop him was to throw salt over your left shoulder. Irish superstition was that if you spilled salt, you had to throw it three times over your left shoulder, or you would be cursed. It is spilling salt that is usually seen as bad luck, and throwing it brings in the good luck.

In Japan, salt is thrown over the threshold of the door to a house after an unwelcome visitor leaves, to ensure that they don't come back. Salt is also sprinkled across the threshold after returning home from a funeral. The salt will prevent any spirits from following you into your house.

Salt was also effective against fairies in Irish folklore. If a child should accidentally fall down, it could be because fairies were trying to run away with them. The child would be given three tastes of salt to drive the fairies away. In medieval times it was a Catholic custom to place salt on the tongue of a newborn baby to protect it until it could be baptized.

On a witch's altar, salt represents the element of earth. When it is combined with water, it is used to cleanse and bless the circle. Salt can also be used in magic as a form of protection, to keep away malevolent entities, or for healing rituals. So really, its current magical uses are very much the same as the historic and cultural uses that humans have always used it for.

There are many types of salt available, and all salt is equally effective, so you don't need to spend extra money on a fancy or rare salt to take advantage of its inherent qualities. A box of cheap, common table salt will possess the same energetic properties as an expensive jar of imported sea salt, but the pricier salt may have some side benefits thanks to its place of origin, colour, or mineral content. The little packets of iodized table salt from a fast-food restaurant can be just as effective in a spell as a spoonful of luxury grade *fleur de sel* from a boutique grocer. There is a type of salt for just about any kind of magic you want to do. It will bring the element of earth to your working and its ability to cleanse, protect, and purify.

Black Salt: There at least three types of black salt to consider, each with their own distinct uses and properties.

1. Black or Witches' Salt: This is not a culinary salt but a salt-based mixture, blended to banish, protect, exorcize, and guard against evil or malevolent forces. It is a mixture used widely in an array of folk magic, hoodoo, conjure, and witchcraft practices. It is popular because it is effective! Sprinkling this around the perimeter of your home will ward off troublesome or uninvited visitors; carry a sachet of it around your neck or in your pocket to shut down verbal attacks, gossip, and malicious bullies. More information and a recipe for Black Salt can be found in chapter 11 of this book.

2. Himalayan Black Salt: this is also called Indian black salt or kala namak. It is a form of Himalayan pink salt that is blended with an assortment of Indian spices, including harad seeds, and then heated. This process darkens the colour to a range of colours from a dark brown to purple, and it can appear pink when it is ground. The harad seeds give it a sulphurous, eggy aroma. Its distinct flavor seasons curries, chutneys, and Indian pickles. It is often used in vegan cooking to add a rich umami flavour.

3. Black Lava Salt: This is sometimes sold as Hawaiian black salt or black sea salt. It is usually made with high quality white sea salt that is blended with activated charcoal derived from burned coconut shells. It has a mild earthy, smoky flavour and is used as a finishing salt, sprinkled on food before serving.

Dead Sea Salt: This salt, as it name indicates, is extracted from the Dead Sea as it has been for thousands of years for medical and cosmetic purposes. It has a different composition than other sea salt or table salt. While these salts are 85 percent sodium chloride, only 12 to 18 percent of Dead Sea salt is sodium chloride. This leaves room for an abundance of other minerals like magnesium, sulfur, calcium, iodine, and zinc.

Epsom Salt: Despite its name, it is not a salt at all; it does not contain sodium chloride. It is the common name given to magnesium sulfate, which does have a salt-like appearance. Epsom salt is a healer, and when added to warm bath water it soothes tired aching muscles and relieves pain. Soaking your feet in Epsom saltwater treats athletes' foot and toenail fungus. It can cool sunburn, treat diarrhea, and boost your immune system.

Fleur de Sel: Called the "flower of the salt," fleur de sel is a highly prized culinary salt renowned for its delicate flavour, light flake, and pure flavour. It is painstakingly harvested by hand between May and September, under very particular wind and weather conditions, from the sea along the coast of France near Brittany and parts of the Mediterranean.

Grey Salt: This originates from France and is harvested from the same areas as fleur de sel. The clay content in the salt flats gives *sel gris* its colour. It is unrefined and slightly moist, retaining all its minerals from the sea. It is a little more expensive than table salt, but the extra flavour and interesting properties make it a worthwhile indulgence.

Kosher Salt: This is a type of coarse salt that is used in the process of koshering meat, a process by which salt is used to draw the blood out of the meat in accordance with Jewish dietary law. It is not the salt that is kosher, but it is the salt used to kosher. This salt not only has this religious significance, but it is also a favourite in most kitchens as it is free of additives and preservatives, is inexpensive, and has a great taste.

Persian Blue Salt: This exotic salt originates from a single mine in northern Iran. The oceans that created this salt dried up more than two hundred million years ago; the blue colour is caused by the presence of potassium chloride in the crystal and extreme pressure. It is expensive and rare, often sold in a mixture with white salt to bring the cost down.

Pickling Salt: This salt is used for exactly what you think—pickling and preserving food. This salt is pure sodium chloride and does not have any additives that can ruin the food you are canning. Additives like iodine or anti-caking agents can discolour your product, make brine cloudy, and cause the dreaded mushy pickles. It dissolves quickly into water, creating a crystal-clear brine that won't discolour your food. I will confess, this is my favourite salt for magical purposes. The connection to food preservation and kitchen witchery gives it an extra earthy edge that is hard to beat.

Pink Salt: This is usually mined from salt deposits in the mountainous regions of Peru and the Himalayas. The colour comes from minerals in the salt crystals or a form of bacteria. The Himalayan version of this salt is the most famous and comes from the Khewra Salt Mine in Pakistan, one of the oldest and largest salt mines in the world. The Peruvian pink salt originates from the Maras Salt Mines located in the Sacred Valley high in the Andes Mountains. An Australian pink salt is harvested from an ancient saline aquifer in the Murray Darling Basin in the southeast of the country.

Red Hawaiian Salt: Also known as 'Alaea salt, it is a sea salt that is harvested from the Pacific Ocean around the island of Kauai. It is said to have the highest concentration of trace minerals and elements of any salt. It gets its colour from the iron oxide-rich volcanic clay that is added to it to give it its distinctive earthy flavour.

Road Salt: This is a strictly industrial type of coarse and chunky rock salt that is used on icy winter roads as a safety measure to melt snow and clear ice off of slippery road surfaces.

Sea Salt: This is usually a more expensive and fancy culinary form of salt. It will usually contain trace minerals that it picked up from the sea water it evaporated from and is either unrefined or only minimally processed so that it can retain its unique character and flavour. Any body of salt water can produce sea salt, but common sources are the Mediterranean Sea or the Atlantic Ocean. It can be purchased in large flakes or finely ground, and it has a clean, bold flavour for seasoning food.

Table Salt: By far the most common, table salt is a highly refined, uniform white salt. This is the stuff you find in saltshakers in kitchens everywhere. It is cheap and multi-purpose, best used for baking and cooking as it easy to measure. It is very high in sodium chloride, as the mineral content has been removed during processing. It may also contain additives such as iodine and anti-caking agents to prevent clumping. For most magical purposes this salt works just fine.

Earth in Alchemy

Alchemy was a form of early chemistry and philosophy by which practitioners hoped to literally and metaphorically turn lead into gold. Within this system are a series of symbols used to represent the elements, metals, and compounds that have been adopted by modern magical practitioners. The alchemical symbol for earth is an inverted triangle bisected by a horizontal line. In this system, earth is believed to possess the qualities of being cold and dry; it represents the manifestation of physical sensations and movements.

Colours of Earth

The use of colour in magic is an important detail that can enhance a magical working by bringing the power of the associations attached to the colour into the work you are doing. The associations a colour carries may vary depending on your Witchcraft or Pagan tradition, and they may also vary by culture and geographic location. Offered below are some examples of colours that are generally accepted to represent earth, along with some general correspondences:

Green: An abundant colour representing fertility, luck, and prosperity. Green is the fecundity of the earth, the generosity of the Goddess, and the colour of nature. It is the colour that represents the heart chakra, and in that system is the realm of relationships and compassion, and what we give to and receive from the world. The heart chakra is the source of the healing energy and our personal authenticity.

Brown: An organic colour representing trustworthiness, dependability, and practicality. It has a rustic charm and comfortable friendliness. It is an unassuming, common-sense colour that is helpful in doing magic related to natural spaces and animals.

Black: Strongly connected to banishing or baneful magics. It has strong protective qualities and is extremely grounding. As the colour of midnight and repose, it is associated with the Crone aspect of the goddess and old age.

White: A colour that shares correspondences with earth, and in some systems is used instead of the more obvious green. It relates to the north, the dark, the land of midnight, and indeed, in northern climates, the very earth does appear covered in white for most of the year.

The Witches' Pyramid

In 1854, the French occultist Éliphas Lévi wrote in his book *Transcendental Magic* about the four "indispensable conditions" that one must possess in order to become a magician. These conditions were summarized as "To Know, To Dare, To Will, To Keep Silence."[3] Subsequent generations of ceremonial magicians and then modern witches have adopted Levi's works, and the conditions that he wrote about eventually became known in witchcraft as the Witches' Pyramid. Each of the conditions was attributed to a different element, with "To Keep Silent" being ascribed to earth.

3   Éliphas Lévi, *Transcendental Magic: Its Doctrine and Ritual* (London: Bracken Books, 1995), 37.

For a magical practitioner, the ability to keep silent has many purposes. There are times when this means to not speak out of turn, and to listen. The power of listening gives us a pause to reflect and listen to not only the wisdom of others, but to the wisdom of our inner voices and guides that may be trying to communicate with us. Sitting in silence and taking in the sounds around you, tuning in to the hum of the natural world around you, can provide comfort and grounding in a stressful world.

Silence is an important ingredient in operative magic. In my coven we try to avoid discussing a ritual or spell for at least twenty-four hours, because we find that if we start to critique or analyze our efforts, we undermine them by overthinking or nit-picking them. What happens in circle stays in circle, and silence about what you did and who you did it with ensures the privacy that builds a strong, intimate working group, and avoids gossip.

Words have power and so does silence. Silence indicates patience, consideration, moderation, and thoughtfulness.

Astrology of Earth

Looking up from earth to the sky at night, we can see the twelve constellations that represent the twelve signs of the zodiac. These celestial signs are broken down into four groups of three signs each. These groups are referred to as the triplicities and each one is associated with an element.

The triplicity associated with earth includes Taurus, Virgo, and Capricorn. People born under these signs are generally dedicated, loyal, and practical individuals with a stubborn streak, a love of comfort, and a need for security.

Taurus: April 20–May 20

The symbol for Taurus is the bull, an animal known for its incredible strength and determination. A Taurean will be loyal and steadfast to the end. They place high value on commitment to friends, family, romantic relationships, and careers. They are in it for the long haul and expect that others will share their values. As a fixed sign of the zodiac, they are the earthiest of the earth signs.

Ruled by the planet Venus, Taurus is a generous lover, a decadent homemaker, and a connoisseur of the finest food, drink, art, and beautiful things. A Taurus must be careful to not overindulge or overspend. They can be prone to profound stubbornness, lack of motivation, procrastination, and possessiveness.

Keywords for Taurus: sensual, stable, materialistic, devoted, uncompromising, and reliable

Virgo: August 23–September 22

Virgo is represented by the image of the Virgin, a female figure bearing a sheaf of wheat that represents the harvest and abundance that their time of year is known for.

Their ruling planet is Mercury, which gives them a disposition toward writing and communication. They are critical thinkers and discriminating in all areas of their lives. As a mutable sign of the zodiac, Virgos are cooperative, team oriented, and flexible people who are able to adapt and accept change.

Virgos are attuned to the needs of others and make long-lasting friendships. The Virgin aspect is represented by the impression of calm self-sufficiency that they project. Virgos have a keen sense of detail and order, which they may take to such an extreme that they sometimes forget the big picture, and can suffer from a sense of never being or doing enough for others or themselves.

Keywords for Virgo: kind, analytical, helpful, reserved, shy, and practical

Capricorn: December 22–January 19

The earthy goat represents Capricorn, a strong, nimble, and grounded symbol for people born under this sign. Their ruling planet is Saturn, which manifests as practicality and responsibility, but also can make them appear distant and cold. Capricorns are hard workers, and coupled with that sense of responsibility they tend to become workaholics or extremely task-focused, and demand that those they are working with meet their standard of commitment to the cause. As a cardinal sign on the zodiac, they tend to make good leaders with strong organizational and decision-making skills.

Capricorns are attracted to others who share their priorities and ambition. They like to make long term plans and finish what they start, and they have a profound sense of guilt when these plans go awry. Tradition is significant and Capricorns can have a hard time changing plans or breaking rules.

Keywords for Capricorn: mature, disciplined, unforgiving, responsible, pessimistic, and independent

Earth Divination and Spirit Work: Earth in the Tarot

The earth element appears in most tarot decks as the suit of coins, disks, or pentacles. In the classic Rider-Waite deck, which would not be so classic without the iconic artwork of Pamela Colman Smith, this suit is referred to as pentacles, so for simplicity I shall refer to this suit as pentacles here.

Pentacles in the tarot is the suit that represents the material reality of life, such as home, career, finances, property, business, trades, and gain. When read in their positive aspect, these cards represent prosperity, comfort, realisation, and manifestation. The negative reading of pentacles reflects the dark side of greed, sloth, over-indulgence, and poor financial management. These cards can shed light on the questioner's personality and motives, revealing issues related to body consciousness, material desires, ego, and self-esteem.

Beginning with the Ace of Pentacles we see the first manifestation of an opportunity to advance in a material way. A new building phase or, if reversed, a warning to not spend frivolously or be greedy. The Two of Pentacles sees us trying to manage our material obligations and juggle challenges before we meet the Three of Pentacles, where we begin to learn how to use and trust our natural talents. The Four of Pentacles is where we begin to save our resources and maybe even hoard them—a reminder to repay debt and appreciate your success so far. Reaching the Five of Pentacles, we are hit with the harsh reality of material loss and inevitable discomfort. The Six of Pentacles can be reassuring that assistance will come, and a benefactor or financing is on the way. Reversed, it can mean you need to concentrate on managing your wealth better and not squander it. Upon reaching Seven of Pentacles, the promise of success is around the corner, but patience is required. Check your expectations and be realistic about where you plant your efforts. With the Eight of Pentacles, we see mastery of skills becoming apparent. Check your ego and remain grounded. Nine of Pentacles is the realization of luxury and extra earning. The dark side of this is a heavy debt load and the loss of comfort. Ten of Pentacles is full realization of wealth and the understanding that this does not mean money alone. Richness in life includes family, friends, happiness, and spiritual fulfillment. The negative side of this is tension and argument that lead to loss of relationships and property.

The court cards tend to be direct references to actual people in your life. The kings and queens usually translate to male and female figures, while pages, knights, princesses, etc., are more accurately read if you consider that they could be people of any gender. Their title refers more to their age and relationship to your life.

The Page of Pentacles represents a young person or child who is wise beyond their age, with a message for you about your material world. They may be dynamic and talented, or greedy and calculating. The Knight of Pentacles is a young adult, usually delivering positive news related to finance and business affairs. They are a champion of the cause, but they may have more self-interest than concern for the best interest of anyone else. The Queen of Pentacles is an accomplished, benevolent, nurturing, and generally maternal older woman. Get on her bad side and she can be stubborn, cheap, and underhanded to gain her much-loved material possessions. And finally, the King of Pentacles, which represents a mature male with power and influence. He is professional and respected in his field and generous with sound advice and support. His downside is that he can also indicate corruption, criminal, or unethical tactics to achieve his end goal.

In the major arcana, the element of earth manifests significantly in several cards. The Empress card is Mother Earth herself, fertile and generous. She is often depicted in a relaxed posture, possibly pregnant, and surrounded by abundance. Ruled by Venus, she offers love, joy, and creativity. In her negative aspect, she can be smothering and possessive, unable to let go, and overbearing. The Hierophant is a card ruled by Taurus, the bull. This card indicates order and institutional systems in progressive working order, and a possible spiritual mentor with well-considered advice. It can refer to various types of contracts, such as marriage or business agreements. Reversed, the Hierophant can be morally judgemental, intolerant, and a departure from tradition. The Hermit is a card ruled by Virgo, the Virgin. Both figures stand alone in forms of purity and solitude. The Hermit is a reminder of wisdom and the value of introspection. He gives sage advice, but only to those who care to actively seek it and who are patient enough to wait for it. In reverse, the Hermit can be absentminded and grumpy, with no time for stupid questions or idealism. And finally, the Devil. This card is ruled by Capricorn, another horned beast. This card forces you to assess your vices and temptations and forces you to confront bad choices you may have made or are about to make. In reverse, the Devil loosens his grip long enough for you to correct a poorly conceived plan or destructive trajectory.

An abundance of pentacles in a reading indicates that there is attention required around your home and work life, and that your material needs need to be attended to. Are your debts paid? Do you feel safe and secure? Is there something you need to do to get your legal and financial affairs in order?

Geomancy

Geomancy is a stream of divination that works through a connection with the inherent energy from the earth and by reading its signs and features. Under this category are a number of systems and practices that all, in one way or another, utilize naturally occurring patterns to create harmony, predict the future, and understand the universe. Some of these systems are sacred geometry, feng shui, tossing coins, rolling dice, dowsing, and the use of mazes or labyrinths. Geomancy is a field of study that combines the mystical with the mathematical and the magical.

Sacred geometry: The study of how geometrical laws affect our environments. Everything manifest in the world, on some level, is composed of structures, patterns, and designs. We can be drawn to certain places or things based on how these things resonate with us on an unconscious level. As human beings began to build structures, they emulated proportions and shapes that were already in nature to create the type of environments that resonated with them. By understanding how to construct them, we can understand the greater design of the universe.

Sacred shapes appear in Witchcraft and Pagan traditions all the time and they hold great power on both conscious and unconscious levels. Some of the most common are:

Circle: Many modern Witchcraft and Pagan rituals and ceremonies are conducted in a circle. It is an inclusive shape where everyone present has equal access to being seen and heard. Circles have no beginning or end and represent unity and wholeness.

Spiral: Moving out from the fixed central point, a spiral implies progression and movement. As the curves wind around the one before it, we see cycles repeating, but with space and distance separating them, implying wisdom and experience gained.

Triangle: A representation of the trinity. In Christianity it is the Father, Son, and Holy Spirit, and in Neopagan circles it can be Maiden, Mother, and Crone. The number three is significant here as well, associated with significant cycles: birth, life, death; and past, present, future; as well as beginning, middle, and end, for example.

Square: Universally a shape of substance, form, and foundation. Order, law, and balance are found in a square, all lines being equal and stable. It is an earthy shape related to the number four, which also corresponds to earth, doorways, practicality, and strength.

Mazes and labyrinths: Created by humans for ritual, decoration, and entertainment for thousands of years. They are usually laid out on the ground using stones, or by cutting the turf to create their shapes. A labyrinth is unicursal—only one way in, one twisting path that winds and loops back on itself, and one way out. They are effective for creating an altered state of consciousness and are suitable for meditation as you walk through them. The same effect can be had using a "finger labyrinth," which is a drawing or model of a labyrinth that you can trace with a finger and get the same result as walking. A maze is multicursal, which means it has a choice of routes, multiple entrances and exits, and dead ends. They are not as meditative as they require more problem-solving. Mazes cut in corn fields or constructed with hay bales are popular family entertainment around harvest and Halloween in North America.

Dowsing: A technique in which you use a tool to indicate when your psychic senses are picking up the signal of something you are trying to find. The most common tools are pendulums or dowsing rods. The tool acts like an antenna, picking the subtle physical and mental messages the user is receiving. The psychic ability, provided it is present, belongs to the user, the reaction from the tool acknowledges and confirms it. Dowsing can be used to find lost objects, to find water sources, or to detect currents of energy found in the earth, known as ley lines. Dowsing rods made of metal are usually L shaped and the user lightly holds on to the short part of the L, with the long part extended forward over their closed fists. Make sure that the rods can move freely and cross in front of you. Next, and most importantly, set your intent. Have a very clear picture in mind of whatever it is you want to find. Then start slowly and evenly walking around. When you get close to your target, the rods will cross. This may take a bit of practice, and you may want to retry approaching your target a few times to confirm success. A pendulum works very much the same way, but can also be used over a map to find lost objects, or to answer yes/no questions. To do this, you can purchase a pendulum, or make one out of a length of string with a small weight tied to the end of it, or use a favorite necklace with a pendant on it. Hold the pendulum in your dominant hand, allowing the weight to swing freely. Start with the pendulum holding still. To "set" your pendulum, close your eyes, and concentrate on a yes/no question you know the correct answer to and make sure the answer is "yes." Open your eyes and note the direction the pendulum is swinging— this will be your "yes." Now do this again and concentrate on a question with a "no" answer and confirm that the pendulum is swinging another way. For me, a "yes" is when it swings back and forth, and for a "no" it swings side to side. One caution: do not get addicted to getting all your answers this way. This tool is only effective when it is not abused.

Chapter 6

EARTH HERBS AND BOTANICALS

Throughout history the image of the witch has been entwined with the magical and medicinal lore of plants. Almost every culture has a reference to the wise one who deals with medicines, or the one who lives on the edge of society, offering cures and remedies for the rest of the community. This knowledge of plant lore comes from taking the time to study and appreciate the signs and signals from the plant realm, and the wisdom that comes from attuning oneself to the quiet signals and messages that the earth provides.

The act of connecting and working with the plant realm is an earth element experience. While some individual plants may have associations with other elements, that practice of tapping the plant kingdom for its power and connecting to the spirits and properties of them is without a doubt a manifestation of earth magic. Some practitioners who specialize in this path may refer to this as Green Magic or Green Witchcraft and devote their energy to understanding herbalism, healing, and the cultivation of medical and magical plants.

The practice of herbalism is an ongoing learning curve, and becoming an adept herbalist is a true commitment. Because herbalism is an unregulated industry with no uniform certification process to determine who is or isn't a qualified herbalist, it is up to the individual to seek the best training and information possible. Many territories have professional associations or guilds that maintain standards and offer codes of conduct. It is advisable to seek these out if you feel a particular calling to professional herbalism, in order to receive the best possible education.

In many parts of the world, it is the Indigenous communities that are the keepers of traditional herbal medicine knowledge. Make an effort to learn who the knowledge-keepers are in your area and how they relate to the local plant medicines. In Canada, where I live, the importance of the relationship between human beings and the land is embedded in the cultures of Indigenous people. Across the country different Indigenous groups have their own protocols and customs for the appropriate use and harvesting of the traditional medicines. These traditions combine a profound respect for Mother Earth and systems for giving thanks for the gift of medicine. Learn where the traditional medicine-gathering areas are in your region and seek the guidance of elders before entering these ancestral places. Some areas may be private, and some may be open to sincere and respectful visitors.

Whether you are harvesting in a remote wild area or your own backyard, the indiscriminate picking of plants and taking more than you need is never acceptable. Tearing out plants by their roots or chopping up an entire plant colony is destructive and disrespectful. You may need to harvest roots occasionally, and these can be carefully done by digging out some, while leaving the rest of the colony intact so that it can grow back next season. Always leave enough behind to ensure that the plants can successfully reproduce. If you are unsure how to do this, do more research and try again later.

While the mastery of herbalism is a huge commitment, this does not mean you shouldn't have a few tried-and-true cures in your repertoire. You never know when you or someone you care about will need a simple remedy and having a few practical recipes and techniques to work with is simple enough to learn. Write these in your journal and note the process and results of your herbal experiences. These notes are extremely valuable to come back to later.

Wildcrafting

There is nothing more rewarding than creating your own medicines from fresh plants that you either grow or wildcraft yourself. There is something so inherently witchy about wandering off into the woods, or your own garden, with pruning shears and a basket, then coming home to get something bubbling and brewing on your kitchen counter.

To wildcraft is to harvest plants from their natural habitat. This can be done just about anywhere that you have wild plants growing. I live in a fairly large city and I often wander down back lanes to walk my dog. I marvel at how many medicinal and edible plants grow along these alleyways, in the cracks between property lines and pavement. Vacant lots, along waterways, and other "no man's land" sites in the city can provide an abundance of interesting and healing plants.

Before you head out to harvest anything, take some time to investigate your area and learn what lives there. Go for walks and take pictures of interesting plants if you can. Use your photos as reference for later research. Read up on the local flora and determine which plants would be useful and practical to you. It is easy to get carried away with wildcrafting and take more than you need, or pick plants that you have no use for, and waste them. Make notes in your journal about the plants you have found, their locations, and the time of year you see them, when they bloom, and when they go to seed. Research before you harvest and, when you do go out and pick some plants, make sure you have the time set aside to process them. Note in your journal the name of the plant, when it was harvested, what you made with it and when it is ready, and how your product turned out.

When you find plants you want to harvest, spend some time observing them first. Is the plant colony healthy? Is it thriving? Do the individual plants look robust or are they pale and struggling? Is this an area that has been sprayed with pesticides or herbicides? Close your eyes and breathe, listen to the sounds around you, and pay attention to what you feel or hear. Is this the right plant to harvest? Ask the plant for permission to harvest it. If it does not feel right to cut it, then don't. Your intuition may be trying to tell you something you need to pay attention to.

There is a wildcrafting joke that goes "all plants are edible…once." Let this be a reminder to not put anything in your mouth unless you are 100 percent sure of what it is and that it will not make you sick or kill you. Another bogus myth is that if you see an animal eat it, it is safe for humans. This is not true. Animals can eat stuff that humans can't and vice versa. Just like you can indulge in the chocolate that can be fatal to your dog, there are things that will kill you that the local critters can eat.

Check out your area for gardening clubs, hiking groups, or wilderness associations, and find out about public events they may offer. I am fortunate that there is an exceptional herbalist in my hometown, and that they offer herb walks and retreats throughout the summer. For a reasonable fee I have been able to benefit from their years of training in herbalism and learn about the plant medicines that are grown within easy range of my own home. The local health food stores in my area also have bulletin boards where I have found notices for interesting events, sometimes sponsored by church groups or environmental organizations, that feature guest speakers giving lectures about everything from butterflies to mushrooms. Not every topic may be your cup of tea, but I can't stress enough how expanding your learning horizons beyond the Pagan universe can enrich your Craft.

Harvesting Dos and Don'ts

- DO only harvest what you need and can process. You can always return for more if you need to.

- DO your research and make sure you know the identity of the plant you are harvesting

- DO NOT harvest from polluted areas. Seek areas that have not been sprayed with chemical pesticides or herbicides.

- DO harvest only from large and healthy colonies of plants.

- DO harvest the parts of the plant you need. If you need the flowers, there is no need to pull the plant out by the root.

- DO be aware of the local wildlife and any risks that it may pose.

- DO learn how to identify poison ivy and poison oak and other dangerous plants in your region.

- DO NOT trespass. Be respectful of the plants and the land they grow on.

- DO be prepared with the equipment you will need to harvest. A good pair of sharp pruning shears, a sharp compact knife, small trowel, a basket or cloth bag, and gardening gloves are essential.

- DO NOT clear-cut an entire patch of a plant. Leave the majority of the community untouched so that it will continue to thrive.
- DO NOT harvest rare and endangered plants.

With these guidelines firmly in mind, go outside and see what is growing in the wilds of your area. My last warning is that hunting and collecting wild plant medicines can become addictive. The thrill of the chase followed by the reward of making your own tinctures, infusions, oils, or balms is so satisfying. I have a small harvesting kit in the glovebox of my car. It is just a pair of gloves, a Swiss army knife, and a pair of pruners in a cloth bag. You never know when you will stumble across something useful and ready to harvest.

Returning to the Earth: Making Compost

To compost is to make an offering of renewal to your garden. Death, decay, and renewal are the lessons your compost pile can help you learn. That fresh, earthy, organic fragrance of rich, healthy soil is largely made up of the scent of decay. When organic matter accumulates on the ground, it does so in layers. Dried leaves and dead plant matter fall on top of living things, which grow on top of dried dead things. This all breaks down together and creates a rich growing medium for more new life to grow up in. This is the magic of composting, and it is easy to recreate this magic intentionally to enrich your own garden.

To get started you will need to decide where you are going to make your compost. You can build a compost bin out of old pallets or scrap lumber. If you go this route, make sure the lumber is untreated, so that you don't have any chemicals leaching into your new soil. Another option is to purchase a pre-made compost bin. The old-fashioned way is to just pick a discreet corner of your yard and make a heap. Whichever method you choose, find a semi-shaded spot that you can easily access, with enough space so that when the time comes to turn or harvest your compost, you can get in there with a shovel to work. One of my indulgent garden purchases was one of those "tumbler" style rotating compost bins that I splurged on at a fancy garden store. It doesn't take up very much space and it is easy to give it a few spins to turn it whenever I dump some scraps into it. It holds heat well, so decomposition happens pretty fast, giving me a good yield of compost every season.

Creating a viable compost pile is very easy to do. You need three elements:

1. Greens: these are your fruit and vegetable kitchen scraps, grass cuttings, coffee grounds, etc. These things provide the nitrogen and moisture that your compost will need to get warm and speed up the decomposition process.

2. Browns: think dried plant matter for this one. Leaves, shredded newspaper and cardboard, chipped branches or twigs, and sawdust (make sure the wood wasn't treated!) will provide the carbon your compost will need. The dried matter also balances with the wet greens, helping your compost to stay damp, not wet.

3. Water: your compost may need a drink from time to time. You want it to feel like a damp sponge, not too wet and not too dry. If it gets waterlogged it can get really stinky and gross. If it dries out completely the decomposition slows right down or stops.

The next thing you need to remember is the ratio. Greens and browns should be mixed about 50/50 in order to maintain a good balance of wet and dry. In the autumn when I rake up the leaves that fall from my oak trees, I pack them into those big paper lawn waste bags and keep a few beside my composter. Whenever I dump a pail of kitchen scraps into the bin, I also add a few handfuls of the dried leaves. If you don't have leaves, hang on to your grass clippings, or try shredded newspaper. Sometimes it's a bit more or less than 50/50, but as long as it is getting a reasonable mix of both green and brown, you should start to see some nice decomposition. Turning the mixture gives it oxygen and speeds up the process. The bottom layers of your compost will probably be ready to harvest first. Dig it out when it has a rich dark colour, and sift out any big pieces of undecayed plant matter. Healthy compost should have that forest floor smell and should also have bugs in it. Don't be worried if you see some worms, sowbugs, or ants in it unless you have an apparent an infestation. Too many of a specific bug means you have an imbalance in your compost and may need to add either more greens or more browns and give it more time to decompose.

A few tips:

- DO NOT add meat, bones, or fats to your compost pile. They will rot and attract pests. Vegetable matter only is the best way to go.

- DO NOT add pet poop to the compost pile! These can contain potentially toxic organisms. Plus, it is just plain stinky.

- DO NOT add synthetic things. Remove those plastic-coated produce stickers from banana peels, and avoid newspaper or cardboard with coloured ink or glossy printing on it. Some tea bags are made out of plastic mesh, so check to make sure that the ones you put in your compost are not made of this.

- DO NOT added diseased plants to your pile. The disease can be spread through the resulting compost.

- DO keep a pail or container on your kitchen counter to collect scraps. Empty it often to avoid attracting fruit flies.

- DO chop up or shred larger pieces of material before you throw them in the pile. This helps it decompose more quickly and easily. Eggshells are great for your compost and better yet if they are crushed first.

- DO sift your compost when you harvest it and throw anything that is still recognizable back into the composter. Sifting does not need to be fussy, just run a rake or your fingers through it to catch any big pieces.

I must admit that I am smitten with my own compost pile. I enjoy tending it and turning it and I love feeding it kitchen scraps and dried leaves. And yes, I do admit that I talk to it. Harvesting the finished compost and amending my garden beds with it to plant new seeds and seedlings brings the garden experience full circle. Last year's scraps become this year's food and plant medicine. It feels very satisfying to take care of my little garden patch this way, and to know that I have taken personal responsibility for a large chunk of the organic waste my household generates.

Gardening for the Spirit

Starting a garden, big or small, and cultivating your own herbs for magical or medicinal purposes is another option. This can be as simple or as complicated as you care to make it. A potted plant on your window ledge is a great way to start and can produce enough to experiment with. If you have the land to cultivate, an herb garden can provide enough bounty to share.

Choosing what to plant in your magical and medicinal herb garden can be an overwhelming task. Where to start? Selecting what to plant should be motivated by practicality. What will you actually use? Included here are some examples of common culinary and tea plants and their magical correspondences, as well as a list of classic "witch plants." The culinary herbs have the advantage of being multi-purpose. You can eat them, and they also have magical properties that are quite helpful. The tea herbs provide medicine, magical associations, and a good cup of tea. Triple bonus! The "witch plants" are not for eating. Some of them do have medicinal properties, but their main purpose is to be used in magic, as ingredients for spells, potions, incense, or some other element of magical work.

Unless you are already confident in your green thumb and gardening skills, start small. Choose three herbs and give them your attention. It is easy to get carried away and dig up your entire lawn, plant one of everything, and then realize that you don't have the time or energy to look after it. Keep track of when you planted them in your journal and document their progress. If you are a tea drinker, pick three of your favourite tea herbs, plant them, and learn everything you can about them. Harvest them and make tea. If you love to cook, plant three culinary herbs and watch them grow. Adding fresh herbs to a salad or scrambled eggs elevates these simple dishes to something special. If you are interested in the folklore around the witch plants, give three of them a try. These can be harder to grow and tend to require more effort. Try as I might to have success with mandrake, they just don't want to flourish in my zone 3 climate. The winter is too extreme for this perennial to survive, and they don't seem to like being trapped in pots and being moved inside when it gets cold. Rue, on the other hand, comes back year after year, growing lush in the summer.

Document the experience in your journal or start a gardening-specific journal. I like to note important dates, such as when I planted something, when it sprouted, and when I harvested it. Weather conditions like rain or drought are helpful to look back on year after year, as are the timing of spring thaw and killing frosts. One last tip, and I learned this one the hard way: draw a garden plan and illustrate where you planted things. Starting a brand new garden with multiple plants is really exciting, but by the time next spring comes around and your perennials start to emerge, you may find yourself standing over a little green shoot wondering what it is.

Culinary Herbs

Herb	Types of Magic	Growing Notes
Basil	Love—has aphrodisiac properties Dried herb can be added to purification incense blends and also prosperity charm pouches.	Annual in most zones
Bay	An effective ingredient in purification and healing blend incenses Burn on its own to promote vivid dreams and visions.	Best grown in a pot in most climates. Keep it indoors during the winter and avoid direct sunlight in the summer.

Herb	Types of Magic	Growing Notes
Dill	Planetary association with Mercury—used in spells to aid communication, learning, and settling disputes.	Hardy, grows tall, good for borders, and self-seeds
Garlic	Planetary association with Mars Leave bulbs of garlic at a crossroad as an offering to Hekate. Hang braids of garlic in the home to ward off malevolent spirits and unwanted energy.	Easy to grow and best sown in the fall for harvest the following summer; a true plant of the underworld
Oregano	Lighter, flowery oreganos associate with Venus and magic related to love. Darker, more bitter oregano is good for protection magic.	Many varieties available, not all culinary; for flavor, try Greek
Rosemary	The old saying goes "rosemary for remembrance"—add dried rosemary to sachets or charm bags for spells related to learning or honouring the dead.	Native to the Mediterranean, it needs warm, dry conditions. It is best planted in a pot so it can come inside for winter in cold climates.
Sage	An earth elemental herb; all varieties are good for grounding and purifying. The earthy fragrance of burning sage for ritual, or cooking sage in culinary use, evokes comfort and security.	Many varieties available, not all culinary

Herb	Types of Magic	Growing Notes
Thyme	An herb associated with air due to its fragrant qualities. Use in spells and charms related to banishing negative thoughts and nightmares, or any magic related to "clearing the air."	Many varieties in an assortment of colours, not all culinary

Tea Herbs

Who doesn't enjoy a nice hot cup of tea? Or a refreshing glass of iced tea? This is the simplest pleasure you can harvest from your herb garden.

The process for preparing herbal tea is very simple:

Using fresh herbs: one tablespoon chopped herb per one cup boiling water

Using dried herbs: one teaspoon of dried herb per one cup boiling water

The herbs can be placed loose in your cup or teapot, then strained out with a sieve, or you can just sip carefully and let them settle to the bottom of your cup. Or invest in a tea ball, fill it with herb, and steep it that way.

It can also be fun to experiment with mixing different herbs to create your own tea blend. My own favourite is one teaspoon dried lemon balm mixed with one teaspoon mojito mint (and those are heaping teaspoons) into my giant mug, filled with hot water and about a half teaspoon of honey. There are no rules to this, you can experiment and make your tea as strong as you want and drink it at whatever temperature you like. It is better to start with boiling water and then chill it if you want it cold; it steeps more efficiently that way.

Herb	Types of Magic	Growing Notes
Anise Hyssop	Protection—burn as incense or plant along property line. Adds a warm licorice flavor to tea.	Perennial; attracts bees and butterflies.
Bee Balm	Calming and clearing—drink before performing divination Associated with the element of air. Adds an Earl Grey type flavor to tea.	Perennial; attracts bees.
Catnip	Planetary association with Venus. Use in spells for love and fertility. Tea is a sleep aid and calms nerves.	Member of mint family; perennial and hardy, prolific grower.
German Chamomile	Effective in magic related to dreams, divination and love. Tea is a sleep aid and wards off nightmares.	Annual; propagates by seed.
Lavender	Planetary association with Mercury. Mix a handful of dried lavender with a cup of Epsom salts to make a healing bath soak. Burn it as a purification incense.	Many varieties available; zone varies.
Lemon Balm (Melissa)	Planetary association with Venus. Deliciously fragrant and effective in spells to attract romance and love. Tea is uplifting and slightly sedating.	Member of mint family; perennial and hardy, prolific grower.

Herb	Types of Magic	Growing Notes
Lemon Verbena	Planetary association with Venus. Effective for use in love spells and to draw the attention of a prospective lover. Adds fresh and fragrant lemon scent and flavor to teas.	Grows up to 6 inches; needs warm climate to thrive.
Motherwort	Use in protective magic, especially for expectant and new mothers and babies. Tea is very calming and helpful for menstrual and menopause symptoms. See tincture recipe on page 232.	Native to Eurasia and naturalized to North America; grows in liminal places and is worth cultivating.
Mint	Use dried herb for healing spells. Anoint wallet with mint oil to attract money. Tea is a digestive aid and anti-nauseant.	Perennial and hardy, prolific grower.
Stinging Nettle	Planetary association with Mars. Very protective plant useful in defensive magic. Add to poppets and charm bags. Tea is a stimulant, but maximum benefit of this nutritious plant comes from drinking an infusion. See page 228 for recipe.	Wear gloves, they really do sting. Drying and cooking neutralizes the problem. It grows wild as a weed but is useful to cultivate.

Herb	Types of Magic	Growing Notes
Valerian	An earth herb—harvest the roots. Add to charm bags and place under your pillow to aid with dreamwork. Use as an amulet of protection against malevolent witchcraft. Tea is a light sedative, useful to calm and to induce sleep.	Native to Europe, naturalized to North America, and is a hardy perennial that grows readily anywhere there is rich soil.

Traditional "Witch Plants"

These plants are considered to be sacred plants to witches for their magical properties and correspondences. Their names are evocative, appearing in magical texts and grimoires. Some of these plants are extremely toxic, so read up on them before experimenting with them. Some of these plants are only safe to consume in small quantities. Rue is one of these and it can be cooked and used sparingly in some dishes. I love growing it and have learned to be respectful of rue's strong and bitter nature. My own experience has been that when I harvest it, I get a mild rash on bare skin, and my heart palpitates when I breathe the freshly cut plant. My witch's intuition tells me that any plant that causes heart palpitations and rashes is obviously a great ally for protection from an enemy or threat. This is not a benevolent plant, but an aggressive guardian from the plant realm.

Spending time with a plant and carefully observing its appearance can give clues to its magical uses. Angelica is a towering plant, growing up to two meters (6.5 feet) tall. Its looming presence in the garden feels very reassuring and protective. Angelica is used in protective charms and powders to repel malevolent witchcraft and evil. It has culinary uses and is hardy enough to grow well in the far north, where it was historically eaten like a vegetable. The stems are sometimes boiled in simple syrup and candied.

I used to live next door to a house that had been divided up into small apartments. The landlord did not live onsite, but he was often around the house, doing yard work, and getting into arguments with his tenants and neighbours. He often rented to some pretty volatile people, and this combination led to quite a few scary situations. I decided to build a strong border of protective plants along the fence that separated our properties. Angelica, monkshood, rue, and henbane were all put to work, lending their aggressive and sometimes toxic natures to shielding my home from the constant battery of trouble next door. Despite the things we witnessed over the fence, and the number of times we had to call the police or fire department, we never had any of that physically spill into our yard.

Plant	Magical Use	Growing Notes
Angelica	Protection, exorcism—mix dried leaves with salt and sprinkle around house to block malevolent magic.	Hardy; grows up to 6 feet tall.
Belladonna (Deadly Nightshade)	Baneful magic; astral projection. Traditional ingredient in flying ointment.	TOXIC: do not ingest; wear gloves when handling.
Foxglove	Baneful magic; divinatory magic. A woodland perennial, it can be used to attract the fey.	TOXIC: do not ingest; wear gloves when handling.

Plant	Magical Use	Growing Notes
Henbane	Baneful magic; trancework; communication with the dead. Weather magic—plant during dry weather to attract rain, or throw dried leaves into water to make it rain. Traditional ingredient in flying ointment.	TOXIC: do not ingest; wear gloves when handling.
Hyssop	A potent herb of purification used in many traditions. Add a pinch of hyssop to a bowl of water to use for ritually cleansing ritual space and participants. Infuse in olive oil to make all-purpose anointing oil.	Tall and showy with little flowers that attract bees and hummingbirds.
Mandrake	Baneful magic. Use in charm bags or poppets for fertility, love, protection. Sacred to goddess Hekate.	TOXIC: do not ingest; wear gloves when handling.
Monkshood	A tall, beautiful, and deadly plant, classic to a witch's garden. Baneful magic. Grow it to honour the Old Gods and the underworld. Traditional ingredient in flying ointment.	TOXIC: do not ingest; wear gloves when handling. Do not grow near plant that will be used for food.

Plant	Magical Use	Growing Notes
Mugwort	Planetary association with Venus. Use mugwort to aid with all divinatory practices. Burn it as incense to enhance clairvoyant powers. Rub fresh herb on scrying mirror and crystal balls to amplify their power, sprinkle dried herb in scrying bowl filled with water to get clearer messages.	Can grow as tall as 7 feet and become quite bushy, so give it space in your garden.
Rose	Planetary association with Venus. Use rose liberally in all magic related to love and passion. Bathe in rosewater to reinforce self-love.	There are many varieties of roses and they all carry the same magical properties.
Rue	This intense herb corresponds with the element of fire and has planetary association with Mars. Use this for active and aggressive protection against both magical and mundane interference.	Grows well in most climates from Zones 3 to 9. It can get quite bushy and dense once established.
Vervain	Planetary associations vary between Mars and Venus, the planets of war and love; beneficial for use in spells related to both things. Can be used in tea for a calming effect, or spells to calm a situation.	Member of the verbena family. Grows well in cooler climates. Attracts bees and butterflies.

Plant	Magical Use	Growing Notes
Wormwood	Planetary association with Mars. Burn as incense to enhance clairvoyance and divinatory powers.	Grows wild in North America and Europe, but worth cultivating a patch to ensure a regular supply.
Yarrow	An essential witches' garden plant, yarrow has many medicinal and magical uses. Add to charm bags and spells for love; throw dried herb across your doorway to ward against negative energy entering your home. Tea made with dried herb, lemon juice, and honey calms a fever. Tea also aids digestion, is anti-spasmodic, and aids menstruation; do not use if pregnant.	A perennial plant in most climates, yarrow can get invasive once established.

A Note About Toxic Plants

Even a harmless-looking plant can cause real harm to a person or animal. The baneful and toxic members of the plant kingdom can be powerful allies and deserve to be included in our magic, but this does not mean we should be disrespectful or stupid when handling them. Do take heed of the warnings and wear gloves when handling these plants. A wise witch is careful, and remember—the properties that make them dangerous also make them effective.

Incense

The use of incense in ritual is usually ascribed to the element of air, but some aspects of incense and incense-making are extremely evocative of earth. Incense is usually made up of resins, which are harvested from trees, as well as flower petals, herbs, and fragrant woods. Each of these will have their own magical and elemental associations. To bring the earth element into your magic via the element of air, here are some herbal and resin incense suggestions:

Amber *(resin)*: True amber incense is made from fossilized tree resin and is the same as the amber used in jewelry. Amber-blended incense is a compound made up of various different ingredients and can be sold under the names "White or Dark Amber," "Honey Amber," or "Golden Amber," to name a few. Both true and blended ambers have strong associations with love, sex, and healing magics.

Burgundy pitch *(resin)*: Harvested from the European Spruce, an evergreen tree, this deep forest-scented fragrance benefits prosperity, healing, and protection magic.

Mugwort *(herb)*: Mugwort corresponds to the element of earth and has planetary association to the Moon. This plant enables us to stay grounded while doing trancework, dreamwork, divination, or astral projection. Use the smoke to cleanse and recharge your divination tools.

Oakmoss *(fungus)*: This species of lichen grows mainly on oak trees, but can also be found on other deciduous, fir, and spruce trees. It is a common ingredient in commercial perfumes, soaps, and scented oils. Its dark, rich, and moist forest scent is beneficial in luck and money spells as well as for grounding.

Patchouli *(herb)*: A scent that is forever associated with the hippie movement, patchouli is an herbaceous, woody fragrance that is deeply sensual. Making the effort to find high-quality patchouli to work with is worth the effort, as cheap stuff tends to be synthetic and chemical smelling. Its aphrodisiac qualities make it perfect for sex magic and love spells. Burn patchouli to commune with earth elemental beings and for spells related to prosperity and money.

Storax *(resin and bark)*: The heady perfume of storax was used in ancient Egypt and Mesopotamia in funerary rites. It is beneficial to burn when doing magics related to the underworld or psychopomp work. The element of storax is earth, and its planetary association is the Moon, so it is a fitting incense for use during divination (especially at a dark moon) and dreamwork.

Vetiver *(root)*: This earth elemental plant is associated with the planet Mercury, which lends it the qualities of being calming, balancing, and helpful to people suffering from nervous problems and flashbacks. Use it for love magic (especially same-sex love) and to attract money and banish thieves.

You may also come across incense sold as "earth blends." These are made up of various ingredients blended to create an earthy scent. Buyer beware, as many commercial incenses are made up of synthetic or chemical compounds that are not only magically inert, but smelly and sometimes even nauseating. When purchasing store-bought incense, read the label to find out what is in them and choose blends with all-natural ingredients. Once you know the difference between synthetic and natural incense, it's hard to use synthetic.

Get Growing!

The information about the various plants presented above is an introduction to the many and various ways you can get to know them and include them in your magic. We are surrounded by the plant kingdom, yet most of us are disassociated from the nutritional, medicinal, and spiritual function they can add to our lives.

Learning about plants—the edible ones, the medicinal ones, and the baneful ones—empowers you as a witch and increases your magical resources, but it also reconnects you to the growing season and to the natural world. A working knowledge of how to forage for wild food and medicine is a practical survival skill, and a tradition that has been almost entirely forgotten in contemporary Western culture. As the world continues to change and global uncertainties increase, we owe it to ourselves and our communities, both magical and mundane, to ensure that we learn and pass these skills along for the sake of human health and food security.

Tree Magic

The relationship between human beings and trees is a profound and intimate one, even when we fail to recognize that it exists. Aside from the material dependency we have on trees, for the lumber they provide to build with and firewood that they provide to warm us, trees provide the most essential component to our lives—the very air we breathe. The oxygen they emit enters our lungs and pervades our bodies on a cellular level. The carbon dioxide we exhale is absorbed back into the tree, giving it life. In a very real way, every breath we take, we take with trees.

With their roots reaching down into the earth and their crowns extending high above, trees connect the earth and sky. They are the pillars that connect the earth element to the element of air. The sounds that trees make come from their interaction with the air, in the form of wind, rustling their leaves or twisting their branches. Each tree is as unique an individual as you are, the patterns of their bark and branches as unique as a fingerprint, yet we tend to see them as anonymous.

I once did an experiment to see if the people in my life could see the trees. At the time, I was living on a heavily tree-lined street, completely surrounded by very large and obvious elms. Over the course of a couple weeks, I asked every guest to my home to look out the front window and tell me what they saw. My guest list included family, friends, coven-mates, and a colleague I was working with on a film about trees. Upon looking outside, everyone would comment on the other houses, the cars, people, or animals within view, but not once did the trees get mentioned. I find it curious that such important figures could be overlooked, but I take this as a reminder of how we take them for granted and of how important it is to talk to people about them and to include them in my everyday life and my magical practice.

The World Tree

Across many cultures, the symbol of the tree is used to represent the axis mundi, or the centre of the world where all levels of existence are joined together. The roots of the tree penetrate downward, to the Underworld, the realm of darkness and ancestors. The trunk of the tree represents the solid realm of the Middle World, our current reality. The branches touch the heavens, or the Upper World, realm of Spirit. The tree is seen as a place of wisdom and a source of knowledge.

In Norse mythology, the world tree is Yggdrasil, an enormous ash tree. Within Yggdrasil are the Nine Worlds, or the worlds of the deities, elements, supernatural creatures, and humans. Yggdrasil is the tree Odin hung from to gain enlightenment. In the Buddhist tradition, it was under a fig tree called the Bodhi Tree that the Buddha sat and meditated to gain enlightenment.

An understanding of trees provides us with a language that can be universally understood to describe human conditions. In his book *Magical Guardians: Exploring the Nature and Spirit of Trees,* writer Philip Heselton says, "The qualities which trees possess—

longevity, inner strength and flexibility, the ability to regenerate and the way they link earth and sky—have made them particularly suitable to act as symbols which help in an understanding of the universe around us."[4]

Ogham

This ancient alphabet is composed of a series of marks running along a central line. It was used to write in Old Irish as well as Brythonic languages such as Welsh or Pictish. It is sometimes also referred to as the "Celtic tree alphabet," as each letter is named after a tree or plant. The original alphabet included twenty characters called *feda,* and were divided into four groups, called *aicme.* A fifth *aicme* was eventually added to the ogham sometime around the sixth century. The origins of ogham are hard to pin down and a definitive answer to this question has yet to be found.

The earliest examples of the alphabet being used date from about the third century CE and are found inscribed on standing stones across Ireland and the west of Britain. I had the opportunity to visit the Ballycrovane Ogham Stone in Co. Cork and had expected this stone to hold some kind of profound spiritual message. The stone itself is thought to be the tallest one in Europe, standing 5.3 meters (17 feet) high. Its placement predates the ogham message carved into it, as it was originally erected in the Bronze Age, and later inscribed with what translates to: "Of the son of Deich a descendant of Torainn." Not the profound message of ancient pagan belief I had hoped for, but an important reality check that not everything from the past needs to be profound to be important. This stone, like many other ogham-inscribed stones, appear to be a boundary

4   Philip Heselton, *Magical Guardians: Exploring the Nature and Spirit of Trees* (Chieveley: Capall Bann, 1998), 57.

marker or a memorial. Or as my tour guide exclaimed, "It's a big stone newspaper!"

In *The White Goddess*, Robert Graves puts forth the idea that the characters of the ogham correspond to a Celtic tree calendar. This calendar begins on December 24, and it includes thirteen 28-day cycles. This leaves one extra day, December 23, which some believe is the extra "day" referred to in "a year and a day":

1. Beith (Birch): December 24 to January 20
2. Luis (Rowan): January 21 to February 17
3. Nion (Ash): February 18 to March 17
4. Fearn (Alder): March 18 to April 14
5. Saille (Willow): April 15 to May 12
6. Uath (Hawthorn): May 13 to June 9
7. Duir (Oak): June 10 to July 7
8. Tinne (Holly): July 8 to August 4
9. Coll (Hazel): August 5 to September 1
10. Muin (Vine): September 2 to September 29
11. Gort (Ivy): September 30 to October 27
12. Ngetal (Reed): October 28 to November 24
13. Ruis (Elder): November 25 to December 22

This calendar also instigated a Celtic-inspired form of astrology that has been adopted by some Neopagans. These proposals made by Graves are up for debate, but they do have an appeal, and some practical applications that work for many people.

The most common modern usage of the ogham is for divinatory purposes. You may see ogham characters drawn on tarot or oracle cards, or on a set of ogham staves. These are wooden sticks, either all made of the same type of wood, or each one can be made from the wood from which the character takes its name. The staves are cut to lengths of four to five inches, stripped of their bark, and sanded; then each one is inscribed with an ogham character. Stave sets usually have all twenty-five characters represented, with an extra blank one added. There are many ways to do readings of the staves. A handy way is to keep them in a drawstring bag. When you want to divine an answer to a question, draw three staves out and toss them on a flat surface in front of you. Your message will be determined by the associations you have with that tree or plant name and how the staves fell in relation to each other.

Shinrin-yoku

In Japan, *shinrin-yoku* is recognized as an effective part of preventative healthcare. Shinrin-yoku translates to *forest bathing*, and it is a widely accepted and prescribed way to reduce the intense stress of everyday life and improve the wellness of Japanese citizens. Scientists at the Nippon Medical School in Tokyo have done research that identifies a nature deficit disorder in modern society and have found that spending time in a forest, breathing the air filled with the natural aerosols emitted by trees, not only releases tension, stress, and anxiety, but it boosts the immune system as well. This research has prompted Japan's Forestry Agency to create and maintain official forest therapy trails across the country, with plans to create many more in the works.

How is shirin-yoku any different than any other walk in the woods? Well, I guess that depends on how you usually walk in the woods. To take full advantage of the medicinal benefit of your time in the trees, let all five of your senses guide you. Try this next time you are in a wooded area:

- Leave your phone, camera, and any other technology behind. We all love to take pretty pictures of nature, but now is not the time. Just be present.

- Don't plan a route, just walk, and grant yourself permission to wander and explore.

- Touch the bark of the trees, smell the flowers, look up into the forest canopy, listen to the birdcalls. If something interests you, spend time appreciating it.

- Change your perspective, adjust your sightlines. Sit on the ground, stand on a tree stump. What changes when you look at things differently? Examine the woodland without judgement, and let your mind wander.

- Breathe deeply, and draw the air right down into the bottom of your lungs.

How to Plant a Tree

Our planet is at a tipping point. Global climate change is happening before our eyes and the enormity of the situation can be overwhelming. It is hard not to feel powerless and unable to do anything to help stop, or at least slow down, the looming crisis. So, I offer you this: there is something quite fulfilling and ecologically important that you can do, and all you need is a patch of land and a shovel. You can plant a tree.

Step One: Select a tree from a local nursery, and please consider choosing a species native to your area. Native trees have the greatest chance of thriving and will help to re-establish the natural local ecosystem. They also provide essential habitat and food for the native wildlife. Take a good look at your space and make sure that the tree you plant will fit, even after it grows up. What do you want the tree to do? An evergreen can provide shade all year around; a fruit tree will have blossoms in the spring and fruit in the summer. An oak is gorgeous but does grow slowly. Think about what would work best in the space and be most beneficial to the environment.

Step Two: Minimize the stress on the sapling when you transport it to your planting site. Wrap it in burlap or blankets for the ride. Ensure the branches are protected and that the root ball is in a pot or at least wrapped up carefully and not allowed to dry out. If you can't plant it as soon as you get it to the planting site, store it upright in the shade, and make sure that you keep it watered.

Step Three: Prepare the planting site. Dig a hole as deep as the root ball and two to three times as wide. Dig up the soil at the bottom and sides of the hole so that it is loose and easy for the roots of your tree to work their way into the earth.

Step Four: Dig some compost into your hole and add some bone meal fertilizer. You can get this at most garden centres, or you can throw in a few washed and clean beef soup bones that have been cut up. This contains phosphorous and will really help the roots develop and get established. Don't go too crazy with fertilizers or extra soil amendments. The tree will do better if the soil is as close to native as possible.

Step Five: Carefully position your new tree near the hole and tip it out of its container. Make sure it is standing vertical in the hole. The top of the root ball should be level with the ground. The point where the roots meet the trunk needs to be at or just above ground level. Burying it too deep can cause it to rot.

Step Six: Fill in the hole with soil and gently press it down to tamp out air pockets and ensure that the tree is secure in its new home. Leave a bit of a depression around the base of the trunk to collect water.

Caring for Your New Tree

Water the new planting as soon as you plant it, and check on it at least once a week to make sure the ground around it is moist. Two or three large buckets of water should do the trick, or you can leave a slowly trickling garden hose near the base of it for fifteen to twenty minutes. If the water is pooling and/or not absorbing into the ground, your tree may be getting too much water.

Some natural mulch around the base of your tree will really help with water retention and weed control; just remember to leave about three inches of space between the mulch and the trunk—piling it too close can cause rot. Do not prune your tree for at least three years unless it has damaged branches or a disease. Let it grow as naturally as possible. Do not worry about staking the tree unless you are planting it in a windy spot or on a steep slope. If you must stake it, make sure that you remove the stake as the tree grows.

Earth Power Trees

While all trees have an obvious connection to the earth, slow-growing hardwoods and trees that bear fruits, particularly nuts, represent the earth element more specifically.

Apple: The fruit of almost any apple tree provides food and abundance for humans and animals alike. Long associated with magic and witchcraft, the apple has been a symbol of forbidden knowledge and immortality in myth and legend worldwide. The Norse goddess Idunn fed magic apples to the gods in order to keep them young forever. The forbidden fruit consumed by Adam and Eve in the Bible is thought to be an apple, a snack that got them banished from the Garden of Eden. We are reminded of the apple's connection to earth when we cut an apple across its middle and reveal the five-pointed star pattern that the seeds create inside.

Cherry: The hard wood of the cherry tree is a much-desired material for fine woodworking and building thanks to its straight grain and smooth texture. The colour and lustre of the wood grows darker, richer, and more appealing with age. In Japan, the blossoms are celebrated with an annual festival. The fast-fleeting and beautiful blossoms are celebrated as a symbol of birth, death, and renewal. The fruit of the tree provides nourishment, and their wood is effective for keeping evil spirits away.

Cacao: This sacred tree brings us one of the most enduring of all comfort foods—chocolate. The Latin name for this plant is *Theobroma cacao*. Theobroma translates to "food of the gods," and cacao is derived from an Aztec word that means "bitter water." In pre-Columbian times, cacao beans were used as currency by Mesoamerican people. It was also associated with death, rebirth, and fertility. The ritual of drinking chocolate was used to bind wedding arrangements and ensure fertility for the couple. The prosperity brought about by trading cacao made it a symbol of power and wealth.

Ivy: Sometimes called English ivy or common ivy (*Hedera helix*), this woody, evergreen plant is not to be confused with the North American poison ivy or Boston ivy. It is native to Europe, Western Asia, and North Africa, and can be considered an invasive species anywhere else it decides to take root. Not a tree in the familiar sense, ivy can grow up to 9 meters tall (30 feet) and may climb other trees or walls for support. They are not parasitic plants, and their clinging does not harm host trees. Mature plants produce wavy wood that is excellent for making wands to work earth magic with. The Roman god of wine, Bacchus, is often depicted as wearing ivy in his crown as it is said to prevent intoxication. It is often used in bridal bouquets as it is believed to also enhance fertility.

Oak: There are an estimated two hundred types of this slow-growing hardwood tree found in the world. The lumber is prized for its strength and durability, despite how difficult it can be to work with. Known as the King of the Forest by the Celts, they called it "Duir" and this is the root of the word "Druid." The oak has been associated with some of the most prominent gods. The Greeks associated it with Zeus, the Norse with Thor, and the Gauls with the thunder god, Taranis. Oaks provide acorns, which are a symbol of unseen and unlimited potential, possessing the ability to become the mightiest of trees. A mature oak can produce up to two thousand acorns per year, but only one acorn in ten thousand will grow up to be a mature tree. An oak reminds us of the earthy qualities of perseverance, patience, and dedication.

Chapter 7

EARTH CRYSTALS AND STONES

The language that describes the crystals and rocks we use in our magical and spiritual practices can get a bit confusing. Quite often the word "crystal" is used as an umbrella term for anything from the "rock" kingdom. It can be helpful to understand the differences between the terms and think about their meanings.

Scientifically, a crystal is a solid substance that has naturally formed into a symmetrical shape, with smooth external surfaces and angles that repeat in orderly patterns. Rock salt is a crystal, and so is a diamond.

Gemstones are usually crystalline minerals that are rare, durable, and processed in order to be set in jewelry or other decorations. Crystal minerals such as rubies, emeralds, or diamonds are selected for their clarity and quality, and are extremely popular. Not all gemstones are crystals. Some rocks, such as lapis lazuli, are cut and polished as gemstones, as well as some fossilized organic material such as amber and jet.

Fossils are the petrified remains or impression of something that was a once living, organic organism. Examples of fossils include amber, ammonite, and petrified wood.

Is there a difference between a rock and a stone? The words tend to get used interchangeably but I find it handy to think of rocks as being rough and in the wild, while stones would be for human extraction or use (think limestone quarry, or healing stones).

It is easy to forget that these precious stones are part of the earth itself, and a natural resource. They were formed when the earth was born, and were created by millennia of pressure, heat, and chance. Once they are stripped out of the earth, they don't just grow back. Each type of stone has its own story and reflects the development of the place that it is extracted from.

Environmental Concerns and Ethics

The interest in and demand for crystals has skyrocketed in the first two decades of the twenty-first century. Celebrity trendsetters have introduced a huge audience of consumers to the healing powers of crystals and spawned a lucrative niche market worth millions of dollars. The exploding interest in crystals and stones has motivated an industry that is unregulated, and it is hard to clearly establish exactly how the stones are pulled from the earth, and who is doing the work.

A large percentage of the crystals mined are the by-product of industrial mining for precious materials, usually gold or copper. To access these commodities, industrial miners will pollute the environment with chemicals and open the ground up with explosives or machinery for open-pit or strip mines. The mining industry is not held to the same rules regarding environmental or labour practices everywhere in the world. In Canada and the United States, for example, there are at least government regulations that they can be held accountable to, but this is not the case in many of the of the countries that are rich in these precious stones. Madagascar and the Democratic Republic of the Congo are both nations that export large quantities of New-Age-shop favourites like amethyst, labradorite, citrine, and tourmaline and do not have the same oversight. Workers are exposed to dangerous conditions and are paid next to nothing for the valuable stones they dig up, and child labour is common.

When not extracted as a by-product of mining, the next category of crystal extraction comes from small operators and family businesses who do the hard manual labour and usually get paid the least amount in the supply chain that leads to the consumer. Most retailers that actually sell the stones have no guaranteed way of knowing exactly how their wares were mined unless they personally go to the source and buy direct, which is not always practical. The largest and most popular trade show for crystals and stones happens every year in Tucson, Arizona, and a huge percent of the stones in North American stores and beyond funnel through here.

I visited a friend who runs a shop that sells jewelry-making supplies, semi-precious stone beads, and crystals. She does personally go to hand-pick her crystals from the small operators in places like Brazil, Madagascar, and India. Her experience has been that these miners work much like small family farms, with everyone in the household participating in the mining of stones. In many of the places she has visited, people are very poor, and mining is the most accessible natural resource that can provide an income stream to the family. To change this system, the entire country and culture would need to change and there is no practical way to do this overnight.

There are ethical concerns about the crystals we use, and it is up to each of us to be thoughtful and determine how we will approach this. Many of the products we purchase also have hidden environmental consequences; from mobile phones to the food we eat and the clothes we wear, everything comes at some kind of unconsidered cost. The best we can do as followers of earth-based spiritual paths is to be conscious and aware of this fact and do some research to learn about the things we are considering buying.

There are many ways to collect crystals and stones without supporting the commercial extraction of new material, but it does take a little bit more work and research:

- Antique stores, estate sales, and flea markets often turn up some remarkable finds.
- Keep your eyes open for thrift store jewelry set with interesting stones. If you don't like the setting, you can remove the stone and use it however you like.
- Check your area for mines and quarries that offer tours and opportunities to dig your own stones. This makes an excellent day out with the kids, or with the coven.
- Organize a "stone swap" with other magical folk in your area. This can be a fun event where everyone brings the stones and crystals they have no use for, and trades them for new ones.
- Try out the local rock you have in the wild around you and substitute it for fancy crystals. Take the opportunity to learn about your local geology and find out how it can work within your practice.

List of Earth Stones

While all rocks, crystals, gems, and stones are parts of the body of the earth and can handily represent the element of earth in magic, some have a stronger symbolic association:

Agate: There are many types of agate and not all of them are associated with the element of earth. Generally, agate is a stone of balance and harmony. It can boost self-confidence and support personal well-being. It heals negative emotions such as anger, bitterness, and heartbreak. Some types of agate that are specifically earth stones are:

- Black and White Agate: A good choice for balancing and grounding the self. When worn on the body it lends protection against physical harm.

- Dendritic Agate: Dendritic means "branched like a tree" which inspires its other name, tree agate. It is a stone with strong association with the ability to connect with the earth and plants. It reinforces stability and a sense of rootedness.

- Green Agate: A receptive, calming stone, it is helpful in settling arguments and aids in decision making.

- Moss Agate: The lacy green patterns within this stone resemble moss, which evokes nature and the forest. It is a beneficial stone for people who work with plants or crops. It attracts wealth and abundance and is helpful for those suffering depression or mental blocks.

Alexandrite: A lucky stone that brings love and creativity to the wearer. It is rare and can be expensive to acquire. Highly effective in spells for creativity and manifestation.

Cat's Eye: This stone will improve your intuition and perception, which is why it is helpful when considering investments or gambling. It does resemble the eye of a cat, so it is appropriate for using as a charm to improve eye health or in spells to "see through darkness." Associated with the astrological signs of Taurus, Virgo, and Capricorn.

Coal: A very humble rock, coal is associated with the comforts of home and hearth and is strongly associated with good luck and money spells. Carrying a lump of coal in your pocket will attract money to replace it.

Emerald: Most popular as an expensive gem, it is also more readily available as a rough unpolished stone. Its rich green colour brings unconditional love, loyalty, and harmony in relationships. It is also very useful in legal matters and business. Associated with the astrological sign of Taurus.

Green Calcite: One of many types of calcite, but the one most associated with earth. In healing, it is a cooling stone and helps reduce inflammation, burns, and fevers. It helps ease transition and gets sluggish or tired people and situations moving again. Also, it can attract money.

Jasper: Another stone with many different types available, jasper is found worldwide and is known as a healing and supportive stone. It is referred to as the "supreme nurturer." Jasper enhances relationships, builds sympathy, and heightens sexual pleasure. Some specific jaspers of earth are:

- Brown: A potent grounding stone, excellent for "coming down" after magical work.
- Green: Excellent for healing magic, particularly for issues with the liver, kidneys, bladder and digestive system; balances ego and restores compassion for others.
- Orbicular: The name is a reference to the appearance of small circles in the stone. Magically it reminds us of the egalitarian nature of a witch's circle, and fairness with all beings. It instills patience and communication. Associated with the astrological sign of Capricorn.

Jet: This is a form of fossilized wood and is not to be confused with "French jet," which really is cut glass. Real jet is a rich black colour and, when rubbed, it can hold an electrical charge. It is a strong protective amulet and can be used to ward off nightmares and amplify psychic awareness. In traditional Wicca, necklaces of jet, or of amber and jet combined, are used to signify initiatory status. It can be found around the world, but some of the most desirable jet comes from the area of England around Whitby. It gained huge popularity in the Victorian era due to Queen Victoria wearing exquisite jet mourning jewelry after the death of her husband. Associated with the astrological sign of Capricorn.

Kunzite: This is a deeply peaceful and tranquil stone. It comes in a range of colours ranging from pale pink to light green and lilac. Kunzite can be worn or rubbed to ease anxiety or stress and is effective to touch or look at when you need to come back down to earth gently. Associated with the astrological sign of Taurus.

Malachite: This intense green stone effectively amplifies whatever energy happens to be around, so bring it out when things are good, but stash it away when things turn negative. It is not a subtle stone at all and may need to be tempered with other calming stones. It is a good amulet for business and trade. Caution: malachite dust is toxic. Do not use this for making gem elixirs! Associated with the astrological sign of Capricorn.

Peridot: This comes in various shades of green and is reasonably easy to find, although gem-quality specimens are much more difficult to obtain. Peridot is effective in the treatment of skin and metabolic issues. It improves mental clarity and awareness. The colour lends it to being helpful in money or material gain spells. Associated with the astrological sign of Virgo.

Tourmaline: Appearing in many colours, tourmaline is regarded as being a strong balancing and transformative stone. It can be clear or opaque and has pronounced striations or a hexagon type structure. It can often be found for sale in natural wand shapes, which are handy for directing tourmaline's inherent power.

- Black: A very brittle type, but very effective for grounding and absorbing negative energy from the environment. It provides a shield against psychic attack or malevolent magic. Associated with the astrological sign of Capricorn.
- Brown: A very down to earth, practical grounding stone. Good for restoring relationships at home and bringing in empathy.
- Green: A stone that brings the energy of the plant kingdom into your magic and opens the heart. It is a constructive stone, focused on progress and creativity. Associated with the astrological sign of Capricorn.

Ready-Made Tools

Some of the stones we use in magic come in the form of ready-made tools or naturally occurring unusual formations. There are stones from myth and legend that are mentioned in magical texts that may or may not actually exist. Here are some you may come across:

Bezoar: These stones were prized by Arabian doctors as long ago as the eighth century CE. They were brought to the West by the twelfth century and were sought as a cure for arsenic poisoning, which was a problem for the nobility of that time. They were also thought to treat leprosy, measles, and cholera. The stones are found in the digestive tracts of animals and people, and they are formed when small bits of plant fiber or a tiny pebble get trapped and coated with magnesium phosphate and calcium.

They are then shaped by the contractions of the stomach muscle. In humans, they can be very painful and cause vomiting and nausea. The ones prized as amulets were usually found in sacrificed or slaughtered animals and were often decorated or set in jewelry. Queen Elizabeth I had one set in a silver ring.

Crystal Balls: The classic tool of divination, what fortune-telling cliché could be complete without a crystal ball? This stereotype is based on the widespread usage throughout history of using these spheres for the purpose of divination. They can be made from glass, lead crystal, or reconstituted quartz crystal. They are not always clear and can be found made of just about any type of crystal. They are used as a focal point for a technique called scrying, or gazing. This takes a bit of practice to do and involves calming and quieting your mind and then gazing into the crystal ball, allowing your eyes to softly focus on the sphere, noting any visions, sensations, or words that come up. These are interpreted as the "messages" from the crystal ball and they come from the subconscious of the reader, not the ball itself. A famous example of a crystal ball can be viewed at the British Museum in London. It belonged to Dr. John Dee, the sixteenth-century astrologer, mathematician, and occultist who served as a trusted advisor to Queen Elizabeth I.

Fossils: These are often used in magic as talismans or amulets for protection and spells related to wisdom, aging, or connection with ancestors or the past. Among the common fossils used in witchcraft are amber, jet, ammonite, and petrified wood. The Museum of Witchcraft in Boscastle has two "Devil's Toenails" in their collection. These are fossilized remains of an extinct species of oyster that, according to folklore, are powerful amulets against painful joints, owing to their twisted shape. The magical associations of the surrounding rock or resin will complement the inherent powers of the type of fossil. Overall, fossils are associated with the astrological sign of Virgo. Because they were once living things that have become part of the geologic record of earth, they are also associated with the element of spirit.

Hagstones: These are also called Witch Stones, Snake Eggs, Holey (or Holy) Stones, or Fairy Stones. They are a powerful protective amulet and are sought out by witches and magical practitioners of many traditions. They are natural stones usually found near water, on a beach, or along a river or creek. What makes them special is that they have a naturally occurring hole right through them. By looking through the hole, you may see the land of Faery, or the otherworld. You can wear it on a cord (particularly a red one) as a protective amulet or tie it to anything else you want to keep safe. As they are stones of earth, shaped by water, they are very effective in keeping sailors and their vessels safe from harm or bad weather.

Pet Rocks: This crazy but true fad of the mid-1970s was a cultural phenomenon. The idea of selling rocks as pets came out of the mind of an advertising copywriter named Gary Dahl. It started as a joke between friends in a bar and blew up into a novelty gift craze that exploded, enabling Dahl to sell around 1.5 million of them in a few short months. They were packaged in cardboard boxes like a pet store would use to send home hamsters, along with a care and feeding manual. Dahl became a millionaire, capitalizing on the human connection to collecting rocks, and silly humour. I had one when I was a kid and I treasured it. It had googly eyes and little silver feet glued on it. It was my gateway into the rock collecting world.

Philosopher's Stone: Medieval alchemists sought the elusive Philosopher's Stone as they believed that it had the power to turn base metals into gold, and that it also provided the key to the elixir of life and the secrets to eternal life. The substance they envisaged may not have been a stone at all; throughout time it was also described as an elixir or a powder. The quest for the stone, and the work done by alchemists to find it, laid down the foundation for the modern scientific method and the disciplines of chemistry, medicine, and physics.

Shiva Lingam: The traditional specimens of these elongated egg-shaped stones are gathered from one of the holy rivers of India, the Narmada. They are composed of a mixture of jasper, agate, and basalt, and colours range from light brown to grey, with reddish stripes or patches caused by iron oxide deposits. Shiva lingam stones are quite smooth due to being naturally tumbled by the flow of the river, and are additionally hand-polished, in observance of Vedic tradition, by the people who collect them. Flooding of the river by a dam project has made true lingams harder to find, but there are alternate sources in nearby mountains for similar stones. Traditionally they were revered as representing the primordial, divine energy from which all life originated. The stones are said to be sacred to Shiva, one of the principal Hindu deities, and the markings on the stones represent the markings on Shiva's forehead. In the West, the shape of the stone inspires the idea that they represent Shiva's phallus. They are widely believed to be a means by which to connect to the Divine. The calming, watery aspect of this grounding stone promotes concentration and meditation. Specimens can be as tiny as half an inch, or as large as several feet long.

Toadstones: In the play *As You Like It*, the great bard William Shakespeare wrote:

> Sweet the uses of adversity.
> Which, like the toad, ugly and venomous,
> Wears yet a precious jewel in his head[5]

The stone Shakespeare is speaking of was said to be a powerful protective amulet and a cure for a wide range of terrible poisons. They were also worn to treat epilepsy and to protect pregnant women from demons and fairies, and their babies from being swapped for a changeling. The source of this gem was believed to be the head of a toad; to be able to take advantage of the powers of the stone, one must extract it from the still-living amphibian. During the medieval and Renaissance periods, toadstones were often set in jewelry, such as rings. Examples of these can be viewed at the Victoria and Albert Museum and the British Museum in London. Lucky for the toads, these stones are in fact the fossilized teeth of a fish from the Jurassic and Cretaceous periods called a Lepidotes.

Viking "Sunstone": This mysterious navigational device was mentioned in the Norse sagas, but little was known about it, or whether it did indeed enable the Norse sailors to navigate by the position of the sun, even when it was obscured by clouds. In the days before magnetic compasses, the sun was an important guide, particularly during the summer when daylight in the far north could last as long as twenty-four hours. The discovery of a calcite crystal known as Icelandic Spar in the wreck of a British ship that sank in 1592 implied that such stones may have been used for navigation after all. Because the calcite has

---

5   William Shakespeare, *As You Like It*, act 2, scene 1, 12–17.

properties that refract and polarize light in a certain way, it can pick up the trace of the sun, even when it is cloudy. It is still uncertain if the Norse sailors did use them as they were shown to do in the popular TV show *Vikings*, but we now know that it could have been possible.

Caring for Your Stones

Each type of stone will have different needs, and from time to time you will want to give them a little attention to ensure that they are clean both physically and metaphysically.

Step One: Cleanse your stones

There are many ways to do this and they all have advantages and disadvantages. Soaking in salt water, holding under running fresh water, or spraying with water are all effective ways, but some stones can actually be damaged or destroyed by water due to their structure, so please do some research on your particular stone before attempting this. Censing stones by wafting incense smoke or burning herbs over and around them works in most cases, as does passing them over a candle flame.

There are some stones that can act as a cleansing stone for the rest of your collection. A favourite of mine is selenite, a form of gypsum crystal. It is translucent and comes in cubes, spheres, or in a natural wand shape. It can cleanse any other stone placed on or near it. Even a small piece added to a bag of crystals will do the trick. Selenite is self-cleaning, so no need to worry about any extra maintenance for this stone. It is also very helpful with general cleansing of the home and personal energy.

Step Two: Charge your stones

Stones can be left in the moonlight to become charged with the powers that you associate with the moon. Leave them directly outside, on the night of a full moon. If outside is not an option a window ledge can work, but leave the window open if possible, so the moonlight is not filtered through glass. Sunlight is also effective using the same technique. Caution is required as some stones, such as amethyst, citrine, quartz, and fluorite can fade from excessive exposure to direct sunlight.

You can also place your stones on your altar pentacle, and let them rest there for a moon phase, absorbing the atmosphere and magic present as you go about your regular practice. If you are doing a working that you don't want to go into your stones, move them out of the area during this work. Another simple way is, if the stone is small enough, to carry it close to your heart, in a pouch suspended around your neck (I tuck them into my bra) and let the beating of your heart and throb of your pulse fill the stone with your own vital life force.

Step Three: Program your stones

If you have selected a crystal to assist you in a particular function or task, it is a good idea to program it for that use. Make sure that the work you have in mind is consistent with the known attributes of that stone, and make your intention clear. A simple way to do this is to hold the stone in your dominant hand and visualize the purpose you have for it. Get a clear picture of the work in your mind and then state your intention out loud. Make a note of when you did this in your journal, along with a description of the stone.

When not in use, dust your stones regularly and consider wrapping the fragile ones up in a piece of silk or other natural fibre. I like to display the ones I have, and I enjoy picking them up and handling them as much as possible. We collect these things for a reason—they are beautiful, tactile, mysterious parts of the earth, and they should be enjoyed.

Chapter 8

EARTH ANIMAL GUIDES

The relationships we have with animals are some of the most powerful and educational ones we have in our lives. Most of us have had an experience with an animal that has left an impression on us, be it a domestic house pet or a wild creature. An animal may take on a deep spiritual significance and become a totem, or emblem, of its perceived power and attributes.

In the archetypal image of the witch, they are often depicted in the company of an animal. Black cats, bats, or toads are common companions. These creatures were often regarded as familiars and were not regular pets. A familiar was historically a demon, brownie, fairy, or imp that could take the form of an animal and assist the witch, doing their bidding and aiding their magical work. These familiars were not mere companion animals, but supernatural beings capable of shape-shifting, and had magical power. They could travel and collect information, acting as spies to find out important information, and report it back to their human counterpart. Familiars were said to have been gifted to the witch by the Devil, or were inherited by their current witch when an elder witch died.

The modern version of the animal familiar is less dramatic. Domestic pets sometimes get elevated to the status of "familiar" by some modern witches. Some see their pets as magical companions, providing a comfort and intuitive sense beyond that of a "regular" pet. The animals that live with us can have an acute ability to detect shifts in energy or "read" a person or situation faster and more clearly than we can. By learning to watch for these signs, we can work with our pets as helpers in our magical work.

Shamanic practices around the world involve animal spirits as guides and messengers that bring protection, healing, and wisdom to the practitioner. Through techniques such as meditation, trance, dancing, drumming, or chanting, humans have developed methods for connecting to the animal world and communicating with animal spirits. This grants the practitioner the ability to access the power and mysteries of the natural world through the filter of their animal guide and all that they represent.

Any animal can serve as a guide, and it is usually a connection that is made spontaneously through meditation, journeying, or dreams. An animal guide chooses you; you do not select it the way you might select a pet. They may reflect a need from your subconscious for some aspect of what the animal is generally accepted to represent. In many traditions if an animal speaks to you, they are your guardian spirit. It may not be a creature that you would choose, but one that carries the message you need.

Types of animals associated with the element of earth fall into some general categories:

- Domestic pets, particularly dogs
- Farm animals such as pigs, cows, and horses
- Beasts of burden, such as oxen, mules, or donkeys

- Burrowing animals like gophers, badgers, and some types of owls
- Antlered animals: members of the deer family (generally only the male animals have antlers, but the females are equally earthy)
- Horned animals: sheep, bison, goats

List of Animals of Earth

Badger: This burrowing animal is a fierce defender of its territory, willing to fight other creatures to defend its turf even against larger and more imposing foes. Badgers are nocturnal, coming out at night to hunt and spending their daytime hours in their "setts." They are surprisingly domestic creatures, keeping their homes stocked with clean grasses and leaves for bedding, and surprisingly tidy.

Bear: An icon of strength, fearlessness, and confidence. The archetypal image of a mother bear defending her cubs speaks of the bear's loyalty to the ones they love and the importance of protecting family and home. Archeological evidence dating back as far as the paleolithic era suggest early humans arranged the bones of bears in caves as part of some kind of ritual. Across northern Europe, bears are associated with shapeshifting and transformation. The ability of a bear to hibernate through the winter and emerge in spring suggests renewal and rebirth. Nanuk is the Inuit name for polar bear, and according to legend they can shape-shift into human form. If hunters are respectful to a dead polar bear, the nanuk will spread the word to living bears, who will then be willing to be hunted.

Bison: In North America, bison once dominated the landscape from as far north as Alaska, right down to the far south of the United States. Massive herds of hundreds of thousands of these animals would migrate across the landscape, grazing on the grasses and plants of their habitat as they travelled. Over thousands of years, the movement of bison helped to shape the ground they walked on. Indigenous people followed the herds, which provided them with food, hides to make tents out of, bones to make tools, and the sinews used to sew with. Successful hunting of a bison meant that the people would have comfort and security. Bison are very protective animals and will work together to keep their young and weaker herd members safe from predators. Despite their massive size, they are agile and can run fast over great distances. They are courageous, fearless, and obstinate.

Bull: Represents hard work, perseverance, protection, and materialistic desires. Ancient cultures in Sumer, Egypt, Greece, and Crete venerated the bull as a symbol of fertility and rebirth. To sacrifice such a valuable animal was to ensure prosperity. Depiction of a sacrificial bull is featured on one of the interior plates of the Gundestrup Cauldron, a Celtic artifact discovered in a peat bog in Denmark. The bull is a symbol of virility, potency, and dependability.

Cow: Most famously considered sacred in Hindu culture where cows are regarded as maternal figures of divine bounty, with their life-giving milk also providing nourishing cheese and butter. Cows are associated with the goddesses Hathor who is often portrayed as having a woman's body and the head of a cow.

Dog: Anyone who has ever loved a dog can attest to the fact that they possess the earthy traits of being loyal, honest, territorial, and amiable. They are pack animals that appreciate social interaction and leadership. Wild dogs will follow the leader of the pack just as our domesticated pets will follow their human leader. Dogs need routine and pattern to thrive. They respect the rules and hierarchy. They are eager to please, and enjoy challenge, play, and entertainment. Dogs are depicted as the companions of the goddesses Hekate, Diana, and Elen.

Goat: The cloven-hooved goat is a symbol of agility, determination, stubbornness, and fertility. They carry a wild energy despite being one of the first animals to be domesticated. Goats were essential to early farmers, providing all the comforts of earth to humankind—food to eat, milk to drink and make cheese with, and hides to make clothing and shelter. They have become one of the most widespread animals, appearing on every continent except Antarctica. Goats appear often in the myths and legends around the world serving deities. In Norse myth, Thor's chariot was drawn by two goats, Tanngrisnir and Tanngnjóstr. Olympian god Zeus was nursed as an infant by the nanny-goat Amaltheia. The Greek god Pan is the lord of shepherds, hunters, and the wild and rustic places. He is well known for his habit of indulging in the earthly pleasures of food, music, sex, wine, and the beauty of nature. Pan has the upper body of a human, and the lower half of a goat. Satyrs are also half-goat, half-man creatures associated with woodlands and lusty behaviour.

Horse: The horse is another domesticated animal venerated for its loyalty and service to humans. Horses provided the muscle and transportation for farming, war, industry, and trade long before machines replaced them. They have the qualities of beauty, grace, nobility, and freedom. Aine, an Irish sun goddess of sovereignty, fertility, and love, is also known as a Faery Queen and can shapeshift into a red mare, which enables her to interact with people on earth. Sleipnir, the eight-legged horse of Odin, is known to be the fastest horse on land and is also able to fly and swim. He could carry Odin safely to Hel and back again. Epona is a Celtic horse goddess who was later adopted by the Romans. Her worship spread throughout the Roman Empire. She is also connected with sovereignty and fertility and is depicted astride a horse, carrying a cornucopia or sheaves of grain.

Hanging an iron horseshoe over the door to your home with the two ends pointing upward brings good luck to the household. It works better of the shoe has been worn by a horse, as it adds the element of protection it gave the animal as well as the positive attributes of the horse itself. It is considered even luckier if you find the horseshoe by the side of a road.

Ox: This beast of burden is closely associated with hard work, tenacity, patience, potency, and strength. In many ancient cultures an ox was a worthy sacrifice to the gods. In the Chinese zodiac, people born under the sign of the Ox are dependable, hardworking, and healthy homebodies with a tendency for structure and routine.

Pig: The earthy pig is a symbol of abundance, agriculture, luck, and prosperity. The Celtic sea god Manannan was said to have a herd of pigs that would be slaughtered, cooked, and eaten, only to reappear the next day to feed everyone again. In the Chinese zodiac, pigs are a symbol of wealth and materialism, but also hard work and good fortune. In ancient Egypt, the pig was sacred to Isis and sacrificed to Osiris.

Stag: The image of the stag is a powerful symbol for many witches and Pagans alike. In many traditions, the priesthood may wear a crown of antlers in honour of the Horned God. Stags are associated with the forests, hunting, death, and sacrifice, as well as fertility, potency, and abundance. They project grace under pressure, vigilance, and adaptability. They have great strength and endurance yet remain gentle and shy. The goddess Diana is often depicted with a stag.

Toad: A symbol of luck, success, and money. In ancient Egypt, toads were regarded as fertility symbols due to their abundant appearance when the Nile River would annually flood and renew the land. The Aztecs associated the toad with the earth deity Tlaltecuhti. They are often portrayed as a goddess but may be dual gender as the representation and reference varies. They are depicted as being a human-toad hybrid, or as an actual toad with a large fanged mouth and clawed feet.

Turtle: In many Indigenous cultures of the northeast parts of North America, the turtle is said to carry the earth on its back. Some versions of the tale tell of a supernatural being called Nanabush, who organized the other animals to swim to the bottom of the sea to bring back some dirt to create the world on the back of the turtle. Other stories say that Sky Woman fell from above and landed on the turtle's back safely. She was so happy that the earth—Turtle Island—grew around her.

Using Animal Parts in Ritual

The use of animal bones, antlers, horns, hides, or pelts in magical practice is as old as the practice of magic itself, and it has seen a resurgence of interest in recent years. Skulls in particular are a popular motif for many reasons, but if you are considering adding these things to your practice, please reflect on your motivation for doing so. Is it to look dangerous and witchy, or is there a spiritual significance behind it? Do the animal parts have a magical function, or is this to look cool on Instagram?

Working with animal parts is not for everyone. The reasons for using or not using these items are extremely personal, and the practice should not be forced on anyone who is not comfortable with it.

Many folks who do sincerely incorporate animal parts into their magical practice tend to see this as a way to honour and work with the spirit of the creature. Their physical earthly remains become sacred objects of veneration and respect. The bones can be effectively used as an effigy or a fetish that the spirit of the animal is called or invoked into. This provides an opportunity to work with a manifestation of the archetypal energy of that animal. It is worth doing some research to learn about the symbolism of the animal you want to work with and understand its habits and behaviours in life as well as any myths or traditional lore that exists about it. Select the animals to work with that are appropriate for the magical work you would like to call on them for. It is important to bear this in mind and not waste or be thoughtless when deciding how to obtain and work with these powerful gifts of the animal kingdom.

The animal parts you use for magical purposes should be obtained in as reasonable and ethical a way as possible. Furs can usually be purchased secondhand, in the form of an old coat at a secondhand store. Hides and leather can often be purchased from a craft shop or, if you live in North America, you may have a specialty store in your area that sells Indigenous handicraft supplies. We have a few of these where I live, and I have purchased complete tanned deerskins for making ritual cloaks for our coven's annual autumn equinox ceremony. The hides are the by-product from sustenance hunting done by local people, and they are sold for a reasonable price through the craft store.

Bones of some animals can be trickier to acquire than others. For bones from animals commonly used as food, you can ask your local butcher if they can save you some raw bones that are left over from their meat cutting processes. These can be useful for making a bone set (see below) or for practicing bone cleaning techniques on. Acquiring bones from non-domesticated animals can be a matter of knowing someone who hunts, or chance. There are also online sources to purchase cleaned and sanitized bones. These can be expensive, and you won't necessarily know how they were harvested.

Animal bones found in the wild should be handled with care. Never touch a dead animal or its bones with your bare hands; always wear gloves. Carcasses can easily be contaminated by a long list of dangerous and potentially life-threatening bacteria, so gloves and a shovel are a must, as is a mask to protect your mouth and nose, and some goggles or a face shield to cover your eyes.

No matter how bleached and clean bones may look when you find them, they will absolutely need to be cleaned, de-greased, whitened, dried, and then repaired of any damage sustained along the way. There are several useful websites and books available to teach you this process and I strongly advise that before you bring home some parts that need work, you do your research and make sure you have the supplies and the fortitude to take the job on. Processing bones can be a really smelly and challenging business.

One last practical tip—collecting dead animals or their parts from natural environments can be considered illegal in some places. Where I live it is considered poaching to remove even a naturally shed antler from a provincial park. It can also be illegal to even possess the remains of certain species. It varies greatly from place to place, so consult your local wildlife authorities to find out what is allowed in your area.

CHAPTER 8

Reading the Bones

This form of divination involves creating a set of small tools to act as symbols and then reading them for messages. As the name implies, most of the tools will be bones, but you may add other meaningful and symbolic items as well. Natural objects, such a shells, pebbles, seeds, or dried roots work really well, but so do manufactured curios like buttons, keys, coins, or dice.

Start by assembling six small bones of different shapes and from different parts of the anatomy. Add in three extra symbolic curios of your choice.

Some curio suggestions are:

Shell: to represent the realm of water, emotions, feelings

Dice: to give you a number. This could mean a date, an age, or a quantity

Coin: "Heads or tails" can represent yes or no

Seed or acorn: new life, fresh start, an idea

Key: transition, doors opening/closing

Crystal or stone: colour and type will determine association

How you correspond each bone to its meaning will be an intuitive process that is completely up to you. I like to think of where the bone came from and what that represents. For example, to me the hollow bone from a bird represents action and movement. Pieces of rib bone from a deer represents the wilderness, gentle strength, and sacrifice.

Once you have the nine pieces of your bone set assembled, put them in a pouch or drawstring bag. Set aside some time and get out your journal to record your notes.

One by one, pull out each piece of your bone set and make notes in your journal of what they represent to you. This will help you establish what your correspondences will be when you use them in a reading.

When you are done, gather up your bone set and put it back in the bag. Meditate on a question you have, and when you are ready, throw your bones. How you do this is up to you. I like to pour my bone set out and let them fall on a square of cloth I have cut to about twelve inches square, with a large circle drawn on it. Look at the pattern the bones make as they fall and make notes in your journal of any immediate messages that jump out at you. I tend to think of any items that fall off the cloth as "out" and don't include them in my reading. Some readers think of items that fall on the left as being "in the past," items in the centre as being "in the present," and items to the right as being "in the future." The circle on my cloth represents a witch's circle, and I read items falling to the "north" of the circle as being messages from the element earth, "east" as messages from the element air, "south" as messages from the element fire, and "west" as from the element water. Bones landing in the centre bring messages from spirit.

Your bone set can be a very personal tool, and how you use them and customize them can change as you grow in the practice of using them. You can add more bones to the mix any time something comes along that just seems to fit. Remember to keep a journal of your correspondences and experiences.

• • • •

Mother Bruin: My Journey Out of the Bear's Den

Working with animal guides is a spiritual practice that human beings have engaged in since prehistory. Bear cults have been documented across Europe by archeologists and still exist today. This essay by Erik Lacharity documents one practitioner's experience with arctolatry, or bear worship. Erik is a Frankish Heathen and he also co-writes *Courir le loup-garou,* a blog dedicated to La sorcellerie traditionnelle du Canada français (French Canadian Traditional Witchcraft).

FOR THE LONGEST time—long before I knew I was a Pagan—I knew that there was something special about the bear—a majestic creature that can be rightfully considered one of the most sacred of all the creatures humanity has ever bonded with. The reasons for this sacredness are easy to see by anyone with even the most superficial knowledge of bears. For one, they are liminal beings. They straddle the world of the seen as much as the unseen. For many circumpolar bear species, they go into their slumber over the harsher winter months, resting within their dens. In the spring, they emerge and roam the green earth. Many of these bears can climb the tallest trees into the heavens above. In the various waterways, whether rivers, streams, or oceans, the genus *Ursus* can be seen joyfully wading about as they fetch a hearty meal. They also have very human qualities about them. They forage for the same foods humans once nourished themselves upon, such as berries, roots, fish, and other creatures. They can also stand upright, have an inquisitiveness about them, and, as many have experienced while coming upon them in the wild, you would almost believe— well, I am convinced of it!—that they can understand human speech.

What has drawn me to my devotion to Mother Bruin—a name I use for her so as not to break *taboo*—is rather the extremity of this liminality that draws her into the mysterious and arcane facets of ancient human religious experience. These extremities are the chthonic *Den* (or cave) and the celestial *Sky*. This is the journey I wish to speak of here. I would also like to take this time to make it emphatically clear that—although I may use comparative research by academics who have studied Indigenous cultures' bear beliefs—I do not use those traditions in my practice. I am ever aware that it is far too easy to fall into the trap of appropriation and for that reason, I prefer to live my relationship with her largely on my own experience. When I feel the need to establish certain limits and frameworks on my *cultus*, I turn to comparatives that attempt to trace back certain religious paradigms of bear worship (arctolatry) back to the earliest human-bear religion(s).

I tend to focus upon papers concerning prehistoric European biomes and societal development as well as folkloric mythemes that have been catalogued across the circumpolar regions of Earth to delineate my beliefs. This sets two extremities for me: the pre-historic, being emblematic of the *Den*; and the folkloric, which fulfills the role of the *Sky*. As extremities go, these periods of investigation—Upper Paleolithic to the Modern Era—span approximately 45,000 years. It is in that place between those extremities that I fill my experience with the experiential. Somewhere between the bear ceremonialism suspected in the Chauvet caves (ca. 35,000 BCE) and tales of the *Bear's Son*, of which there are hundreds of European and North American versions, I find myself as the interlocutor living the mysteries these two points provide. It is through experimental archaeology (making tools and items from the past in a contemporaneous way) and deductive reasoning that I have come to the conclusions I have. From here on I will paint you a picture of my practice.

I have come to believe that the world follows a cyclical narrative that is painted in the *Sky*. Yet, up until recently, humanity had never physically been able to access the *Sky* other than through ritual. Therefore simple-yet-complex rituals were needed to access the heavens. It was upon the walls of the *Den* where early humanity would *paint the Sky*. That is to say, the processions of the stars, weather, and seasons. Just as the seasons process, so does the Big Dipper (often believed to have been a Bear). She—Mother Bruin—emerges from her *Den* in the spring with her cubs (in various folk tales a warrior son and a healer son). She is hungry, thirsty, and protective. In the summer the *Dipper* comes down and begins to fill, and by the fall she is in her *fullest* position. In the coming of winter, she is seen to enter her *Den* only to emerge once again ... and the cycle continues. This celestial drama—which is macrocosmic—is drawn down onto the *Den* wall. As the interlocutor, we give her worship through this divine emulation.

Through ochre and charcoal, we renew the celestial tapestry of the *Sky*. Through the consumption of her meal—foraged foods— we offer her and the cubs nourishment. Through masked processionals and dances—similar to, but organically distinct from, those of the Pyrenees peoples—we dance the dance that takes us from the *Den* to the *Sky* to unite with her. Her songs are *Emergence, Transformation, Death, and (Re)birth—all* to the beat of the seasonal procession. Many others whom I have discussed *in situ* modern arctolatry with have expressed these same feelings they have received from the Bear: She at once gives birth and subsequently devours. The *Big Dipper* emerges, devours, and so transforms, and then the death of the summer's tide is born in winter. The cycle is ever continuing and balanced.

I find myself giving thanks to her for the changing seasons, for the fullness of my stomach, the *Den* within which I am sheltered, and the mysterious teachings she and her procession can reveal to me. Within her warm chthonic and earthen layer, I am born—just as the cub. I am weary of *Father Bruin* who may drive me from her side. I sing the songs she has given me and make offerings to her imagery, *painting the Sky* in my *Den*. Through my processionals, I climb the *Tree*, which will unite us in the stars here and ever after. I invite others drawn to her majesty to listen to the seasons and follow her on this sacred journey.

Erik Lacharity

• • • •

The Animal-Human Bond

The intense connections we have with animals goes beyond the mundane world and crosses over into our dream and spirit worlds. They appear and reappear alongside humans throughout time as our teachers and companions. Some animals have allowed themselves to be domesticated because they see something that they need in us, just as we see something we need from them. This goes beyond and deeper than the obvious need for food and survival. There is a resonance on a magical and spiritual level that most humans are too busy and too distracted to tune into.

Animals associated with the element of earth share so many qualities and attributes that humans also appreciate, such as domesticity, loyalty, hard work, nurturing, and companionship. We are more like our animal guides and pets than we think.

PART
3
∾

RECIPES, RITUALS & SPELLCRAFT

Chapter 9

CONNECTING WITH THE SPIRIT OF PLACE

Folk who practice magic tend to try and live in tune with the natural cycles of nature. Magic requires a sense of attunement with the natural tides and energy in the environment and a sympathy with the natural forces, both seen and unseen, that surround us. This often manifests in how a witch relates to the land they live on.

For some this may mean having an animistic view of the world. This is the understanding that everything found in nature is, in its own way, sentient and has a soul, life force, or supernatural power. An animist would see the land around them as a fully animated and living place, full of spirits and divine energy emanating from everything, from the smallest grain of sand to the largest mountain, all plant life, and all creatures. Some may even extend this animism to constructed things, such as buildings or even mechanical things, or items of technology, such as cars or computers. By acknowledging and recognizing this force in the world around us, we come to a closer relationship and respect for the land and everything connected to it as a living entity. The land begins to take on personality and character that we as humans can better relate to.

The immanent life of the land around us has been named many things by different cultures. In Norse mythology the land spirits are referred to as *landvættir* or "land wights." These spirits have the ability to help or hinder humans and are sensitive to the treatment that the land and its creatures receive from humankind. They can be communed with to recruit their support as helpers or allies, but this is a reciprocal relationship so, in return for their aid, offerings such as food and drink must be left out for them. Care must be taken to ensure that good relationships are maintained with the *landvættir*, so it is important to explain to them any plans you may have to alter the environment.

In ancient Rome, the belief in the *genius loci*, or spirit of place, was common and we still use the term today to describe the indwelling spirits of a specific location. Examples of Roman altars to a genius loci have been uncovered that depict figures holding cornucopias or offering bowls, indicating abundance and fertility. One particular example at the Corinium Museum in Cirencester, England, includes an inscription that translates to "To the holy genius of this place" and also includes a hollow on the top to hold sacrificial offerings. Across the Roman Empire, a multitude of different genii locorum existed, each very specific to a particular area and reflecting the spirit of that place.

Folklore from southeast Asia tells of spirits of place that must be appeased in order to be allowed to use the land that they inhabit. To disrespect these spirits will bring ruin and destruction to the person responsible, so in order to maintain a good relationship, people provide spirit houses for the local spirits to live in. These small replica houses are beautiful and elaborately decorated shrines that are set in front of a home or business either on the ground or on a pole. Traditionally these are erected when a new building is created or a new business opens, to give shelter to any local spirit that may be dispossessed by the new construction. Spirit houses also provide a place where offerings to the spirits may be left. Food, candles, flowers, or incense are favourite gifts for the spirits, and they will bestow prosperity and happiness on the household or business in exchange for daily offerings. This is a living tradition still practiced by people of Asian descent today. Even where I live in Canada, spirit houses are found in the front entryway of Asian grocery stores or restaurants, adorned with burning incense, and food.

Before you try to build a conversation with the genius loci of your own area, you will need to do some research and give some thought to which spirits you want to connect with. It is important to not be idealistic and believe that all spirits of place want a relationship with humans. Some may be hostile, or just want to be left alone. Some may not recognize you or your offerings and others may see you as a threat to their own habitat and well-being. When dealing with nature spirits we need to respect that some of them have been attached to the land since long before human beings showed up and they may not care about our offerings, magic, or success. Try to imagine what the relationship might look like from a non-human perspective. What benefit will the spirit receive for helping you? Are the offerings you may be able to provide of any real value to the spirit?

Land spirits are inherent in the folklore and cultures of Indigenous peoples around the world. In North America, South America, Australia, and New Zealand, for example, spiritual and religious relationships exist between Indigenous people and the spirits present in the land. These relationships represent a living tradition that has been kept alive despite the challenges and hardships faced by Indigenous communities as they have been invaded by colonists who have stripped them of their land, culture, and identity.

We are at a point in history where the discussions on how to constructively live together and heal the damage done by the last five hundred years of conquest and colonialism are just starting to happen. Within modern Pagan and Witchcraft forums, the debate and discussion surrounding what constitutes cultural appropriation is an ongoing conversation that needs to be addressed by every practitioner. We have an opportunity and obligation to audit our own practices and behaviours and ensure that we are building our own traditions on a foundation of respect and consideration for the communities that may be hurt if we take their rituals, symbols, medicines, and practices without the contextual understanding and training to fully appreciate their depth and significance to the people they belong to. In many instances, these things are being taken without permission and are exploited for profit and personal gain. We can do better than this.

Land Acknowledgement

A land acknowledgement is a statement that is delivered at the beginning of an event or public gathering to identify Indigenous land and to draw attention to the rights of the Indigenous people who live on this land. Across Canada and Australia, and to a lesser extent in the United States, these statements are usually the first thing spoken at official gatherings, such as government, academic, and community meetings or events. As Pagan and Witchcraft groups are becoming more aware of the importance of supporting Indigenous communities, land acknowledgements are being incorporated into public Pagan celebrations and stated at the opening of rituals and circles. By speaking a land acknowledgement before a ritual, we show respect to the Indigenous people, who are the traditional stewards of the land, and to the local land spirits, who have been present long before the arrival of colonists and settlers.

Writing a land acknowledgement takes some thought and some research. If you live in a country that was created on Indigenous land, this process will help you build a clearer understanding of who the ancestral custodians of the land are and how they came to be displaced so that your current community could be created. Writing and then using this statement does not equal venerating the spirits of the land; this is meant to be a show of solidarity and support and also a way to educate other Neopagan practitioners about the history of violence and colonialism perpetrated against the people whose land we now occupy. As Pagans and witches, we hold the land as sacred, alive, and infused with spirit, yet we rarely reflect on the effect that the pain and suffering inflicted on the Indigenous people has on the land itself. If we are reaching out to the spirits of these lands with offerings, prayers, and reverence we need to also reflect this respect in how we relate to the Indigenous people that have been in a relationship with those same spirits for millennia. It is also crucial to remember that these cultures and relationships are alive and well in the present; they did not end when colonists arrived, despite efforts to erase them.

• • • •

Indigenous Perspectives on the Land and Pagans

Guest essayist Karen Froman is a member of the Six Nations of Grand River, Mohawk Nation, and a history nerd. She is a lecturer at the University of Winnipeg, where she teaches the histories of Aboriginal Peoples of Canada and the History of Indigenous Education and Residential Schools.

Ske:kon neechies! When I was asked to write this piece, I admit I did hesitate a little bit as I sometimes encounter hostile resistance and as an Indigenous woman, I am tired of this. However, an Indigenous perspective on issues of land and spirituality is important in a settler-colonial world.

I am an urban, mixed-ancestry, cisgender daughter of a residential school survivor. My mother is of Irish, English, and Dutch ancestry and my father was a proud but hard Kanyen'kehaka (Mohawk) man. He, along with his younger sisters and brother, was taken away from his family at the age of nine and placed in the Mohawk Institute residential school in Brantford, Ontario. When my father entered this place, he spoke three languages—Mohawk, Tuscarora, and English—and had begun to learn the traditional teachings from his father. When my father left the school, he spoke only English and had effectively been brainwashed into believing he was less than Euro-Canadians. This odd sense of shame and pride in our Kanyen'kehaka heritage was passed down to my sister and myself, but due to the residential school violence and abuse experienced by my father and aunties, they were unable or unwilling to teach us anything about our heritage.

As a person of mixed ancestry, I grew up feeling as if I didn't "belong" to either culture, that I was "placeless," without an identity or culture I could claim as my own. By the time I was fourteen I had discovered Wicca. This was mainly due to the fact that it is easier to find information about a European form of reinvented ancient spirituality than it is to find information about a specific Indigenous culture. Most of what I was able to find in the 1980s that purported to be Indigenous was, in fact, random teachings from across Turtle Island presented by non-Indigenous sources. For me, my practice of Wicca was a personal and private thing, although I did wear a silver pentacle necklace as an identity marker.

This pentacle was bought when I was fifteen years old and never came off.

When I was twenty-seven, I was a newly divorced mother of two toddlers, and I had only a Grade 10 education and my job skills consisted of slinging beer in nightclubs. I entered university as a mature student, and this was the first time I was exposed to large numbers of Indigenous peoples outside of my family. For many of us, university or jail, which are colonial institutions, are where we first encounter our true histories, cultures, spiritualities, and languages. In university I finally had the teachers and the ability to come to understand who I am and where I belong. As I learned about things such as the Indian Act, treaties, reserves, the outlawing of our ceremonies, and residential schools, things about my family and the way I grew up started to make sense. I suddenly understood why my father and aunties were unable to pass the teachings down, why there was so much chaos and violence, and why I felt so lost. For many years I had followed my mother's ancient Celtic path because it was easily accessible, but it had somehow never felt quite "right." As I went further in university and decided to major in Native Studies, I began to actively seek out traditional teachers and Elders who could help guide me.

In my third year of university, I took a formal course on Indigenous spirituality and traditional teachings that was taught by a Faithkeeper. One day, as we were sitting in circle listening to a traditional Kanyen'kehaka story, I suddenly felt all the hair on the back of my neck stand up and I somehow "knew" how the story ended and what the message was. Our Faithkeeper stopped in mid-sentence, looked at me and said, "you know how this ends, don't you?" I simply stared at him in shock as he laughed and continued the story. Later, he told me what had happened was "blood memory" asserting itself. When I arrived home later that day, I absentmindedly scratched my neck and realized that while the silver chain was still there, the pentacle that had not left my neck for thirteen years was gone. I came to understand that the pentacle was gone because it didn't "belong" to me and I was on the "wrong" path. I'm not saying Wicca is wrong, simply that it was wrong *for me.*

As many of our teachings and traditional ways were violently torn from us via the schools and the law, today we are trying to reclaim and rebuild. When we see non-Indigenous peoples taking our teachings, our medicines for their own, or worse, for profit, we see the ongoing disrespect and violence of the settler population. These teachings, the land, the plants, the waters are all sacred to us no matter which Indigenous nation we belong to. Most important is the land. Literally everything in the Indigenous world comes back to the land, both in the past and still today. We are connected to, and a part of, the land in deep and profound ways that are difficult to explain.

When we see non-Indigenous peoples selling bundles of sage and sweetgrass or charging exorbitant fees for a sweat lodge "ceremony" we are appalled. This is really a form of theft because these teachings and medicines do not belong to you, the settler population, and were never meant to be sold for profit. Many of the ceremonies and how to conduct them are special knowledge, not "common knowledge." We do not believe that any ceremony can be done by anyone who feels like it. The same thing goes for the medicines. We see many of our picking spots have been picked clean by non-Indigenous peoples, which is something we would never do. When picking medicines, we always leave an offering of tobacco to give thanks, and we leave some to grow next year. Further, many medicines should only be picked at certain times of the year, or the day, and in certain ways. All of this is stuff you simply cannot learn from a book or a website or a "weekend retreat." This is stuff you learn after years and years of face-to-face teachings with Elders and traditional teachers.

Another teaching I have been given relates to the land and ceremony. I have been taught by many Elders that the spirits of the land that we call Turtle Island do not "recognize" the settler population, in that the land spirits do not know who you are, and you do not carry that "blood memory." If this is truly your land, as settlers, then where are your stories? Your stories are across the waters, your spirits of the land are across the waters, and some of the traditional teachers I have learned from do not believe your spirits can cross this water. So, when you hold your own reinvented Pagan ceremony on this land, the spirits of this land will not hear you. When you call your spirits here, when you summon those ancient European spirits, some say they cannot come here because of the waters. I am personally not so sure about this, and I worry that this Pagan practice is simply yet another form of colonialism, another way for the settler population to take what does not belong to them. So, if you must insist on these kinds of ceremonies, then I respectfully ask that you send your spirits back across the water when you have done your ceremony.

We do not forbid non-Indigenous peoples from coming to our communities, to our ceremonies, to our gatherings. In fact, we welcome your participation because this builds understanding between our two peoples. What we do object to is the taking of these things as your own. Thanks, nia;wen!

Karen Froman, Kanyen'kehaka Nation
• • • •

CHAPTER 9

Writing a Land Acknowledgement Statement

A land acknowledgement does not need to be long to be effective. The crucial thing is to speak it from the heart, with respect and accurate information. Here is the one I wrote for my coven to use at the beginning of our rituals:

> We stand now on Treaty One Territory, the ancestral land of the Anishinaabeg, Cree, Dakota, Dene, and Oji-Cree people, and the homeland of the Metis Nation. We give thanks for the gift of clean water, supplied to us by the land and people of Shoal Lake 40 First Nation. Before we invite the deities and elemental spirits of our tradition to this circle, we wish to show our respect to the spirits of this land, and assure them that we meet with peace, friendship, and a commitment to ongoing healing, justice, and reconciliation with the traditional people of this land. (lay out offering)

There are three main points to research and consider:

1. Learn about the people and history of the land you are on. Find out how to correctly spell and pronounce the names. Is there a treaty in place? Was the land ceded or unceded? Build your own understanding of these things so that you can be informed and able to share this information accurately with others.

2. Examine your motives for writing this acknowledgement and think about the context in which you will use it. Do you have a sincere concern for correcting and healing the conflicts of the past? Will you use this statement at the beginning of a public open circle or a private ritual? If you are being insincere in making this statement, the spirits and the people listening will pick up on that. Choose your words carefully and be prepared that some folks may not appreciate or understand why you are

doing this. Your research should be able to help you give informed answers.

3. State your purpose and include words about how you plan to create a better future. This is an opportunity to express how the circle or group participating in the event can build their own constructive relationships with the land, the spirits, and the Indigenous communities concerned.

This process may be difficult. None of us that are colonists or settlers on traditional lands want to think of ourselves as "bad" or as disrespectful to Indigenous people, and the politics involved can be very complicated and confusing. Many of the mistakes made by well-intended practitioners come from ignorance, so educating yourself is very important. Start with writing down what you already know and then do your own research to fill in the blanks. For those of us who do come from settler and colonial backgrounds, this is an opportunity to objectively look at our own attitudes, educate ourselves, and come to a deeper understanding and relationship with Indigenous communities and by extension, the land spirits we claim to honour as witches and Pagans. If we really feel strongly that the land is sacred, we must remember that the land connects us to these people and spirits.

After you have had a chance to research and think about these three points, write a land acknowledgement of your own that summarizes what you have learned. You may need to revise it periodically, as your understanding grows, and depending on your audience.

There is work that everyone can do, even people not living on Indigenous land. All our cultures can contribute to healing the history of violence and colonialism:

- Do not take Indigenous practices, symbols, or systems and exploit them for personal gain. If you have a genuine calling to these things, learn from authentic practitioners the appropriate ways of dealing with them. Before you use or take something, ask yourself honestly—is it yours to take?

- Do not use an Indigenous sacred site for Neopagan rituals. Do not remove offerings or artefacts you may come across when you visit sacred places. As much as you may appreciate the energy or aesthetic of that space, to do this would mean you are walking into someone else's traditional and sacred space and appropriating it. If you feel strongly about that particular location, learn more about it from authentic sources.

- Do not assume that reading a book or doing a Google search constitutes having first-hand knowledge of the experiences of Indigenous people. What settlers and colonists can learn from the stories of Indigenous people does not compare with the lived experience and blood memory of Indigenous people. Make space for these voices to be heard.

- Never assume that there is one homogeneous Indigenous culture. Each tribe, nation, or group is separate and distinct, with as many similarities as there are differences. What may offend some may be perfectly fine somewhere else, so before assuming, ask respectful questions.

- Do not romanticise the past. Movies, TV, and books have told us stories about "Cowboys and Indians," savages, and brutal primitive people. This propaganda often portrays the European explorers and settlers as heroes, bringing civilization to the New World and providing culture to an empty land. This erases the history of conquest and violence that actually happened, and that we all need to acknowledge.

At this point in history there are more questions than answers in how to heal these wounds and live together respectfully. We have an opportunity to open the dialogue and speak to these issues directly, and the connection witches, Pagans, and Indigenous people have to the land gives us a meeting place to work from. If everyone who views the land as sacred can extend this to all beings that share it, and actually live that way, we have a real shot at the better future we all hope for.

Chapter 10

BURIAL AND DIRT MAGIC

Placing an object in the ground is an act of transformation and sacrifice. The practitioner creates something and gives it up to the earth, wishing for a boon or request to be fulfilled. The earth receives the object and transforms it. The offering may rot, rust, decompose, or melt into the ground. As it does, the intent of the object is communicated to the earth energies required to do the work and grant the request. Working this closely with the actual earth is messy, visceral, and primal. You are interacting with the living planet in an intimate and personal way that will directly tap the cycle of birth, life, death, and renewal.

Burying objects for magical reasons has a long history and fortunately enough archeological evidence has been discovered that we can get a pretty good picture of what the magical practitioners were doing and how they were doing it. In ancient Rome, curses were written on lead tablets and then either buried in a grave or tossed into a well. A collection of curse tablets at the Johns Hopkins Archaeological Museum includes one that explicitly describes a curse directed at an individual named Plotius, who was to be cursed with terrible fevers. The person who wrote the curse addressed it to a pair of underworld deities, Proserpina and Pluto, and to Cerberus, the three-headed dog who guards the gates to the underworld. These tablets are believed to have been originally placed in a grave, as it was believed that the soul of the deceased would be the messenger to take the curse to the deities that had been called upon.

Witch bottles are a type of protective and defensive charm that originated in Europe and have also been found in North America and other places that Europeans immigrated to. Historically these bottles were counter-magic, used to deflect malevolent magic being hurled at the victim. The bottles were buried in the ground outside the home, along property lines, under the threshold of the front or back door, or laid down under the foundation of a new building. They were sometimes "buried" in an obscure corner of a building, such as up a chimney, under a hearthstone, in a remote corner of the attic, or sealed up in a wall.

Many examples of witch bottles have been discovered in Great Britain, and one fine example is housed at the Museum of Witchcraft and Magic in Boscastle, England. It was made using a Bellarmine jug, a type of salt-glazed stoneware that was popular in the sixteenth and seventeenth centuries, and features a face embossed on one side. It contained fingernail clippings, bird bones, a red hand thought to be made of coral, pins, and a braid of white hair, possibly human. This would have served as a counter-curse to prevent any nasty witchcraft from entering the home it was concealed in. It was found within the walls of a house that had been bombed during World War II, and based on the evidence seems to have been put there sometime between 1895 and 1912. It is interesting to note that the jug was already old when it was put to use as a witch bottle.

Archeology often provides us with a glimpse into the history of witchcraft. When unusual objects are found on a dig, and no obvious domestic or industrial use can be ascribed to them, they are often written off as "ritual objects." In 2003 an excavation at Saveock, in Cornwall, England, unearthed what turned out to be, over time, a series of "witch pits." These burials had been placed in the ground over a long span of time, from at least the seventeenth century until modern times. I had the unique privilege of being able to visit Saveock and meet Jacqui Wood, the archeologist who discovered them, in 2016. I was allowed to view many of the artefacts that had been uncovered and many of them are consistent with the sort of items that would be used in a witch bottle, but the extensive use of animal parts and the way they were so carefully and deliberately arranged in the pits was truly astonishing. A tremendous amount of thought, care, and in some cases risk were taken to create these mysterious burials and it was apparent that some highly focused magical work was involved in creating them.

Burying is best performed outdoors, in the natural earth, but this can be problematic if you don't have access to secure, private land. If this is the case, fill a large flowerpot with clean, organic potting soil and designate it for this purpose. In a pinch, small items can be tucked in with a potted houseplant. Be careful to remember that the plant will need water, and this may interfere with the item you have put in the soil. Outdoors can also be a problem if you live in a place that freezes and becomes covered in snow. The freeze-thaw cycle can cause the ground to expand and contract, get waterlogged, or heave and this may damage objects buried in the ground. Depending on the reason for burying an item, this can be a good or a bad thing, so plan ahead.

Reasons for Burial Magic

Cleansing: This is an energetic cleansing rather than a hygienic one. Ritual tools, particularly the ones associated with earth, such as your pentacle or the bowl that holds salt, are good candidates for burial cleansing. If you are burying an item that is delicate, water soluble, or contains iron, it should be protected from water seepage and from being stomped on or crushed. Crystals and stones are excellent to cleanse this way. The earth is their natural element and returning to the source cleanses and recharges them with natural earth energy. Make sure that any crystals you bury are not affected by water. A soaking rain can potentially damage a water-sensitive stone, such as selenite or chrysocolla.

Protection: Magic that is done to deflect or protect from evil or negative forces is sometimes referred to as apotropaic magic. Creating or obtaining a magical object and then burying it on or near the person, place, or thing you want to protect is a traditional form of apotropaic magic. One common form of this is a witch bottle, as mentioned above. The corpses of domestic pets, usually cats, were used to ward off evil, and were buried near an opening in the building, under a doorstep, within a wall, embedded in the foundation, or bricked inside the chimney. The cat corpses are often naturally mummified by the time they are rediscovered, thanks to the dry and relatively airless cavities they are entombed in. Shoes were very common to bury or conceal in the walls of a structure for protection. It was very popular in Great Britain and this custom spread around the world. The Northampton Museum has a register of more than 1,900 shoes that were found concealed in buildings, mostly in the UK, but they also have entries from Canada, the USA, Poland, France, Spain, and other parts of Europe. The original reason for using a shoe is unclear, but some theories about this really resonate. Shoes hold the shape of the person who wore them and hold their essence. This could act much like a witch bottle, attracting and trapping any malevolent energy directed at that person. Many of the shoes found to date belonged to children, and it is thought that these were used as children are innocent and pure and their shoes would reflect this. Or maybe it was because they outgrow their shoes faster making it more practical to use.

Absorbing: Dirt can hold "memory." It has the ability to pick up the energy from the objects, structures, living things, and events that are on or in it. You may choose to bury an object so that it may absorb the energy of a particular place to imbue it with that associated energy. For example, selecting a sentimental object that represents home and then burying it in your front yard for a period of time would be a strong talisman to carry against becoming homesick while travelling. Collecting the dirt from significant places for magical purposes is also extremely powerful. In African diaspora traditions, graveyard dirt is used for its powerful connection to the energy of a burial. The knowledge, charisma, and talents of that buried individual are "remembered" by the soil and can be channeled into magical use by collecting the soil, and then using it in magical work requiring that energy. Sprinkling dirt over an object to pass the energy into it can be as effective as burying the object in the soil. It is a matter of what is more practical at the time.

Communication: The earth can become a conduit of communication with the spirits of the land and life on it. You can do this by writing a message on a piece of paper or creating a magical object with a message to a particular spirit in it and then burying it so that your message can be absorbed by the ground. The same idea can be used for sending messages to the underworld or ancestral spirits. Messages as well as offerings, preferably bio-degradable ones, can be committed to the earth, which will in turn transform and transmit them.

Cursing: Writing down the details of a curse and then burying it is a magical practice that has a long history. The lead tablets mentioned above provide a great example of how this can be performed, and you don't need to use a lead tablet to do it. Carving your message on a piece of clay or writing it on paper can also be effective. The important thing is to put some effort and focus into what you are doing. Your magic will only be as effective as the thought and intention you put into it. If you are truly interested in cursing someone, make sure it is for a damn good reason, and be prepared for any consequences that may boomerang back at you. If this is directed at another magic practitioner, they may very well detect what is happening and send it right back at you, so really think on it before you act. I am a firm believer that there is a time and a place for cursing, but it must be well considered and thoughtfully planned.

Manifesting: Is there something you want to see grow in your life? Write what you want to manifest on a piece of paper or create it symbolically out of biodegradable material. This should be reasonably small, something you can fit in the palm of your hand. Dig a hole in the ground, or a pot of fresh organic potting soil, and drop your paper or object in. Cover it with a layer of soil, and then add a few seeds or a baby plant and cover it accordingly. Water your new plantings and take good care of it. Visualize that thing you wanted to manifest growing as the plant grows. This type of spell takes some time to work because it needs the time the plant needs to "take root." For this reason, it is better to plant something that grows quickly. Flowers like nasturtiums or sunflowers work well, or herbs like basil or cilantro should all germinate and sprout within seven to fourteen days and come to a mature size within weeks. Planting an acorn and waiting for a mature oak, well, that would be a lifetime.

Making a Witch Bottle

Creating a witch bottle is a very hands-on, tactile experience. Collecting the various pieces that will make up the witch bottle should be a very focused and deliberate action. The purpose of this is to protect the person(s) and/or place intimately connected to the bottle and neutralize the incoming threat.

Find a Bottle

Start by finding a glass bottle with a tight-fitting cap or stopper that appeals to you. You want a bottle that won't leak! It can be any type of bottle, but glass or ceramic work best and would be considered more traditional. Please don't use plastic! Something on the smaller side, with a one- or two-cup capacity is most practical. Filling a gallon jug, particularly if you choose to use urine as an ingredient, may not be as fun as it sounds. Make sure the mouth of the bottle is wide enough to fit the objects you choose.

Gather the Ingredients

Next, gather the solid ingredients for your witch bottle. Remember that you are creating a "trap" for the negative forces that you want protection from. Your trap should contain elements that lure the negative force, and then imprison it so it can do you no harm.

Suggested solid ingredients include:

- Bent pins
- Rusty nails
- Broken glass
- Barbed wire

- Fishhooks
- Razor blades
- Thorns
- Salt
- Ashes
- Tacks
- Red thread, tangled
- Baneful herbs
- Rust

Decide on what you want to use to bait the trap and link your bottle to yourself. The idea is to put something of yourself into the bottle, so that the malevolent energy is drawn to it, instead of you. Nail clippings, hair, blood, semen, and urine will all work just fine. Blood and semen are extremely potent for magic, so just a few drops will do. If you choose to add blood, your local pharmacy will sell lancets, those sterile single use needles used for doing blood tests. Pricking a finger and collecting a few drops will work just fine. Wash your hands thoroughly first and have a sterile bandage ready for when you are done.

Nail clippings and hair can also just be a small amount. A few strands of hair can be plucked or cut from your head, or a quick trim of your finger- or toenails will work very well.

For the liquid ingredients, urine is easy enough to collect and symbolically it seems to fit. I imagine it like a "pissing contest," as demonstrated when one dog pees over another dog's pee to exert dominance. If you can't manage using urine, then vinegar, red wine, or seawater can be substituted. The idea with the liquid is to swamp or drown the malevolent energy. Use just enough to top up your bottle after you have added your solid ingredients. The last thing you will need is a candle or some wax you can melt to seal the bottle.

My coven once got together to make witch bottles for some protection work we were doing. We were each responsible for making a bottle. We drank big cups of tea and then we each took turns slipping into the bathroom to collect our urine. We were very focused on the task at hand and were working outdoors just to be sure that if there were any spills, they would be absorbed by the grass, instead of the carpet. Upon returning from the bathroom with a plastic beer cup full of pee, my coven-mate said with a grin, "Well—if you aren't up for peeing in a cup, this witchcraft may not be for you."

Craft Your Witch Bottle

Have all your witch bottle parts gathered together in your working space. You can craft your bottle as part of a ritual, or just go ahead and make it, but it is advisable to take a moment, at least, to ground yourself and focus your intent. It can be as simple as this:

Close your eyes and place your hands palms down on your worktable or altar.

Take some deep breaths and let your mind clear. Allow your face to relax and be aware of how your body feels. Give yourself a couple moments to stretch and feel comfortable. Open your eyes and pick up your bottle. Visualize the place and/or people you are going to protect. Start packing the bottle with the ingredients you have chosen. Take your time and make your movements deliberate.

Leave enough room in your bottle for the liquid you will be adding. I like to fill it no more than one-third to half full of my chosen ingredients.

If the malevolent energy that you are concerned about is a specific person or thing, you can add a symbol representing it to your bottle. This can be a photograph or a piece of paper with their name or a description of what it is. Tear it in half and roll it up before tucking it in the bottle.

Now add the liquid. This is where a funnel comes in handy. Carefully pour in your urine, vinegar, wine, or seawater—or a combination of those things. Put the cap or stopper on the bottle and make sure to tighten it.

The final step is to melt enough wax to seal the bottle up so that nothing can leak out. You can either light the candle and let the wax drip down over the cap, molding it with your fingers while it is still warm, or you can gently melt wax chips in a small saucepan over low heat on the stove. Move the saucepan off the heat and carefully turn your bottle upside-down and dip it into the wax allowing it to cool between dips until your bottle has a good seal on it.

You may also want to decorate your bottle with signs or sigils using paint. You can drip more wax on the bottle and use it to stick baneful herbs or thorns to the outside of the bottle.

Burying the Bottle

The final step is to bury your bottle. Historical witch bottles have been found buried under the thresholds of houses, under hearths, and inside walls. This is probably not an option for most of us, but it gives you an idea of the importance of hiding it somewhere safe and getting it into the ground. If you have land attached to your home, you can bury your bottle in a far corner of your property, or in a strategic spot along a property line or some other liminal, border-like space. I have planned my witch-bottle-making around garden renovations, such as having a new fence built. I had some small ones ready to go in the ground when the fenceposts were being set, in deep post-holes. This ensured that they were down deep and along the surveyor's lines that marked the legal boundary of my property. If an outdoor burial is not possible, bury it in a plant pot, and place it by the main door to your home.

Some folklore says that it should be buried upside-down, to further confuse evil spirits, and some suggest right-side up, so nothing can leak out. Trust your own intuition and place your bottle in whatever way feel right given your circumstances.

The protective powers of your bottle will be in place for as long as it is hidden and unbroken. You may choose to dig it up and remove it when you sense there is no longer a need for it, or if you move. This is up to you. I choose to leave the ones I have buried. Maybe I just get a chuckle out of knowing that maybe someday, someone will discover it, and be intrigued to know what it is, and who put it there.

I was once giving a talk on spells, and the topic of witch bottles came up. I described the traditional types of ingredients like rusty nails, broken glass, and pins, and suggested that a witch bottle should contain nasty things for the malevolent energies to "step" on. There were a few grimacing faces and exclamations of "ouch" as I spoke. As I paused to catch my breath, one of the women participating, who happened to be the quietest, sweetest, and most unassuming of the group, said in a deep voice, "I would put Lego in the bottle." This cracked everyone up and we all agreed—it is the quiet ones that are the most dangerous.

Graveyard Dirt

The use of dirt from a graveyard for ritual purposes dates back to ancient Egypt and is an ingredient used today by practitioners of African diasporic religions, witchcraft, and folk magic. The idea behind using the dirt is that the energy and wisdom of the person buried in the ground has permeated the soil around where they lay. When a person dies, their soul may move on, but their talent, knowledge, and strengths are remembered by the body committed to the earth. When we collect this earth, it becomes a power ingredient for magical spells.

To collect graveyard dirt, you first must identify which grave you want to collect it from. The grave of someone related to you, or whom you admired in real life, would be a good place to start. The traits of a person will help you determine the use for the soil. For example:

- If your great-grandfather was a war hero who earned many medals for bravery, dirt from his grave would be appropriate for protection and courage spells.

- If your late great-aunt was a successful medical doctor, this dirt would be appropriate for healing spells.

- If you are lucky enough to go on a pilgrimage to the grave of your favourite author or musician, this dirt would be appropriate for creativity spells.

Upon reaching the grave, spend some time communing with the spirits there. Reach out to the spirit belonging to the grave you want dirt from and ask permission to take it. If it doesn't feel right, don't do it.

You will only need a small amount of dirt, enough for a small jar or bottle, so arrive prepared with your container and a spoon or small trowel. You will also need to bring something to leave behind as a gift or offering to leave at the grave in exchange for what you are taking. This is common across the traditions that use graveyard dirt and must be observed. Customary items from the abovementioned traditions include rum, whiskey, coffee, coins, flowers, incense, or tobacco. You may have knowledge of a particular favourite thing that the deceased would appreciate and choose to leave that.

When digging out your dirt, ensure that you are not taking or damaging any of the plant life that may be present, and cut a small hole in the turf, carefully pulling back the sod. Scoop out only what you need. Tuck your offerings into the hole and replace the sod. Depending on how busy the cemetery is with other living people, you may want to bring some flowers with you. Fussing with flowers over a grave is such a normal thing to see at a grave that you should be able to discreetly take some soil without attracting attention. When exiting the cemetery, you should walk backward out of the gate, or turn around three times before leaving. This is said to confuse any spirits that may be trying to follow you home.

Your bottle of graveyard dirt is potent, so you will only need a pinch or small spoonful for most spells. You can add it to poppets, charm bags, or witch bottles. Sprinkling it around the outside of your home keeps unwanted visitors—visible and invisible—away from your door. A bowl of it on your ancestor altar at Samhain will aid in communication with the dead.

There are many tradition-specific customs attached to the collection and use of the dirt, so if the idea of this practice compels you, it is worth doing some additional reading and research.

• • • •

The Saveock Pits

Buried objects for magical purposes have been found all around the world, but none are as captivating as the burials discovered by archaeologist and researcher, Jacqui Wood. The "Witch Pits" were discovered on her own land, in Cornwall, UK, where she has been living, digging, and experimenting with ancient domestic techniques for more than thirty years. She is also the author of several books and research papers, including *Prehistoric Cooking; Tasting the Past: British Food from Stone Age to Present;* and *Cliff Dreamers*, an adventure series set in the Mesolithic era.

I FIRST DISCOVERED the pits while excavating a Mesolithic clay platform on my land. The platform, which dates to 10,500 BP ("before the present"), is artificial and laid onto peat over a spring line. This was to create access to fishing at the river's edge and to make a place to put up seasonal dwellings next to their fish traps. This is, I feel, very significant, and is the reason the pits were dug into this area, because the clay made the ground wet and the only plant that thrives there is the soft rush or *Juncus*.

I think that there were two reasons the pits were deposited there: one, because they were on top of the energy of the spring line; and two, because digging a pit in the rushes and putting the rushes back on top makes it impossible to see that anything was deposited there. The rushes are typically found on wet areas of fields and are usually fenced off by farmers, avoided by people walking, and not built on. Therefore, the people depositing the pits could be very confident they would be left undisturbed. Also, due to the wet conditions, the contents of the pits would be well preserved (which they are; the feathers still look new, even though they date in some cases to 1640).

Undisturbed, that was, until I came along and removed all the soil down to the clay in the whole area, excavating the Mesolithic camp meticulously. It was not until 2003 that we came across the first pits, which were rectangles, roughly 36 cm long and 27 cm wide, cut into the clay platform. When we dug into the pit, we started to find feathers attached to the sides.

The first suggestions about the pits were that they were just plucking pits (when a farmer plucks a bird for the table, he does it into a pit to contain the feathers and dispose of them). However, on closer inspection we found the feathers were still attached to the birds' skin, which was laid skin side down and made a beautiful, neat feather lining. This then overruled the plucking pit idea, as the tastiest part of a bird is usually the skin when cooked, and no farmer would waste such a resource.

The first pit we found was lined with brown feathers like those of a buzzard or hawk that still fly above the valley today. At the base of the pit was a pile of small water-worn stones mixed with different types of bird claws. The next pit was lined with white feathers, which we had identified as swan feathers and down. This changed our opinion about the pits completely, because it has been illegal to kill a swan in Britain since the twelfth century, as all wild swans are owned by the crown and a couple of dukedoms.

We contacted the Witchcraft Museum in Boscastle, which is described as having one of the largest collections of witchcraft-related curiosities and ephemera in the world. When one of the directors of the museum came to look at the pits, he said he had not seen or heard of such practices before and did not think they were very significant; he likened them to witch bottles dug into the ground.

To cut a long story short, by 2019 we have excavated fifty-five pits. Quite a number had been emptied in antiquity, leaving just a trace of feathers, stones, or fur to indicate their original contents. Each of the pits has a pile of the tiny stones in it, which we had analyzed by geologists; they determined that the stones came from a lake fifteen miles away. So, we knew then it was not a practice just local to this valley. Most of the pits were rectangular, and either north-south or east-west aligned; there was only one round pit that was excavated. This pit was lined with swan feathers, and on either side of two magpie birds were fifty-five eggs, seven of them with baby chicks ready to hatch in them; this pit was dated to 1640. For a group to risk killing a swan and burying fifty-five eggs, seven with chicks ready to hatch, was a serious and generous commitment to their belief system.

By 2008 we started to find animal pits: a cat pit lined with cat fur had cat claws, teeth, and a whisker on the fur, and a large piece of quartz was laid halfway up the pit. This quartz was holding back twenty-two eggs, all with baby chicks ready to hatch in them. That pit was dated to 1740. Then there was a pig pit and a dog pit. The dog pit held the skeleton of a dog laid over its own fur that lined the pit, with the cooked bottom jaw of a pig between its legs; this was dated to post 1950. This was taken up by the world media, ending up with a National Geographic TV documentary based on the pits.

The latest date for the pits was found in 2010 when I excavated a pit and put it on YouTube, as I excavated it unedited (Saveock Pit). This was lined with two kinds of goat fur, with the four legs of a kid laid at the bottom. The jaw of the goat was at one end, set on a piece of plastic with orange bailer twine around the neck. This type of twine was not invented until 1960, and was not used in Cornwall until 1970. So, there is no doubt in my mind that this previously unknown belief system is still very much alive in Cornwall and still a practice only known to those who participate in it.

A pit we did not have a date for was next to the egg and magpie pit, and it had cygnet feathers in it. A student, when cleaning the pit, took a bit too much off and discovered a pile of very degraded printed paper behind the feathers. For two years, every time it was too wet to dig, my students would with tweezers and magnifying glasses try and find a word on the printed paper that would give us a date for the pit. Then eventually we found it! One word that I feel conclusively tells us when the pit was cut, and it was "Mussolini"! So, a civil war pit was put next to a World War Two pit.

The most puzzling thing I found though is the layout of the pits in the marsh. It would have been important during the British civil war when witches were hunted to leave no trace of an offering pit. As I said previously, when you replace the rushes on top of the pit it completely disappears. If quite a number of pits have been emptied in antiquity, how did they find them again? They would not leave a stick or marker, as that defeats the object of keeping them secret.

The really extraordinary thing about the pits is that this belief system has been practiced in my valley for more than 350 years, and yet it is not written about anywhere. Usually, maybe after a family rift, someone might tell someone "yes, my family dig pits," etc., which is how most practices become folklore and are catalogued over the years by academics. It is the first example of an unknown belief system being discovered wholly by archaeology.

People often say to me, "Don't you want to find out who they are?" I always say no. I respect their beliefs and have no desire to find them, so their pits are safe with me looking after them.

Jacqui Wood

• • • •

The Magic Under Our Feet

There is a t-shirt I occasionally see folks wearing at Pagan gatherings that says, "Pagans: We literally worship the ground you walk on." There is much evidence that this is true! From the actual soil and stone, to the strange and wonderful artefacts that may be buried in it, there is much to learn about and do with the ground right beneath you. Do not take for granted the inherent magical qualities of the earth, sand, dust, and grit on the ground. It has a life and energetic force that can enrich your magic, protect, create, destroy, and remember.

Chapter 11

EARTH RITUALS AND SPELLS

There are many ways to incorporate the element of earth into your magic. Rituals can be focused on an earthy subject: healing, finances, career, or home and hearth. Spells can incorporate earthy components such as salt, dirt, stones, bones, sand or plants. Magics that manifest material goods or summon earth energy and direct it toward a goal are also considered earth magic. You may use a pentacle to charge an object, share ritual food or move your physical body to the earthy beat of a drum. Making something within sacred space, a charm bag or mixing up a jar of black salt, is also a manifestation of earth in your craft. Being mindful of your magical footprint on Earth by using natural, biodegradable materials whenever possible in your ritual and spell work is the very least any practitioner of magic can do to give back to the planet that sustains us and provides the energy and inspiration for our practices.

A Ritual to Consecrate a Pentacle

To consecrate a magical tool is to dedicate it to its magical purpose, cleanse it of any prior energies and attachments, and prepare it for its new purpose as a sacred object and magical implement.

Once you have either acquired or created a pentacle that you like, it is time to formalize your relationship with it by consecrating it and putting it to work on your altar.

INGREDIENTS:

> Your new pentacle
> A bowl of salt
> A bowl of water
> Earthy incense
> Candle to represent North (earth coloured)
> Candle to represent Fire (red, orange, or yellow)
> Statue or symbol of Earth Goddess
> Statue or symbol of Earth God
> An amount of ritual food, such as small cakes or biscuits, so everyone present can have some, plus one portion for the gods
> Your journal

Begin your ritual by setting up your altar or working space with the items listed above, and any other items that represent earth to you and help enhance the mood. This may include items such as a potted plant, rocks or crystals, and deity statues.

Orient your setup so that as you perform your ritual you face the north. Place your pentacle in the centre of your altar. Arrange the salt bowl, water bowl, incense, and fire candle around it. Light the fire candle. Place the north candle in the north of the altar and leave it unlit for now.

If you are using self-lighting charcoal to burn loose incense, light it now.

Begin by positioning yourself at your altar, facing north. Close your eyes and ground yourself.

Once you are confident that you are well grounded and ready to begin, light the north candle and say:

"Spirits of the north, element of earth! I call you here
from the depths of the planet, from the mountain
caves and verdant valleys. I call you from the time of
midnight and the darkest night. Bring your ancient
wisdom and powers of growth, abundance, and fertility
to bless and consecrate this rite!"

Turn your attention to the Earth Goddess statue or symbol and say:

"Great Earth Mother of All Things,
I call on you to nurture and guide me as
I do bless and consecrate this symbol of earth."

Pause for a moment and let your words sink in. Then turn your attention to the Earth God statue or symbol and say:

"Great Father of the Land, I call on you
to protect and witness me as I do bless
and consecrate the symbol of earth."

Pause for a moment and then pick up your pentacle and hold it with both hands. Feel how solid it is and trace its lines with your fingers. When you have committed this tactile experience to your memory, light your incense.

Pass your pentacle through the incense smoke and say:

"By the power of the element of air, I do bless
and consecrate this pentacle and blow away
any pollution that may bring harm."

Pass the pentacle over the candle flame as closely as you can without burning yourself or it, and say:

"By the power of the element of fire, I do
bless and consecrate this pentacle, and burn
away any foulness that may bring harm."

Use your fingers to sprinkle some water on the pentacle and say:

"By the power of the element of water, I do bless
and consecrate this pentacle, and wash away
any impurities that may bring harm."

Pick up a generous pinch of the salt and rub it on both sides of the pentacle and say:

"By the power of the element of earth, I do bless
and consecrate this pentacle. As earth meets earth, earth
creates earth, ensuring a strong foundation
for our work, rich in the nourishment our
magic needs to be successful and true."

Hold your pentacle over your head and say:

"In the names of the Earth Mother,
and Father of the Land, I bless and
consecrate this pentacle. So mote it be."

Place your ritual food on the pentacle. Using whatever technique you are comfortable with, raise energy and direct it into the food. Share this small feast with any other attendees, reserving a portion to place outside as a ritual offering to the gods.

When your feast is done, extinguish the fire candle. Thank the Earth Mother and Father of the Land for their presence. Take a moment to reflect on how their presence was felt in the ritual.

Place your pentacle in the centre of your altar, make sure to dust off any crumbs, and take a moment again to trace the lines of it with your fingers and feel the weight of it in your hands.

Look to the north candle and say:

"Spirits of the north, element of earth! Thank you for attending this rite. Return to the depths of the planet, to the mountain caves and verdant valleys. Return to the time of midnight and the darkest night. Your ancient wisdom and powers of growth, your abundance and fertility were well received and appreciated!"

Blow out the candle. Take the ritual offering outside and leave it near a tree or rock if possible. If going outside is not an option, keep it wrapped up in a biodegradable wrapping until you can.

Home Closing Ritual

Moving to a new home can be an overwhelming experience. It can be hard to leave behind a place that holds happy memories and deep sentimental attachment. Packing up material goods is one thing, but how do you transfer the energy and spirit of a place?

This ritual should ideally include everyone who lives in your household. You can expand this to include anyone who is a frequent visitor. It is a fun ritual for kids, and a good one for those non-Pagan folks who may live with you. You don't need to cast a circle, and you only need a few simple, easy-to-acquire items.

Not all homes are happy ones. Before you begin this ritual, you must focus on only taking with you the positive energy and memories of the place. In an extreme case, you may have nothing you want to carry forward. If this applies to your situation, see the note below.

INGREDIENTS:
　　A candle in a fireproof container you can carry around
　　Candle snuffer (if you don't have a candle snuffer, you can use a spoon instead)

Incense in a container that is safe to carry around (stick or loose incense work equally well)

Household members or regular visitors to act as helpers

Start by opening every interior door inside of your home. Open all closets, cupboards, crawl spaces, etc. Weather permitting, open all the windows. Turn on every light in every room.

Gather your helpers together in the room at the highest point in your home that is the farthest away from the front door. For example, if your home has an accessible attic, start there. If you live in a single floor bungalow, or apartment, adjust accordingly. The point is to be as far away from the main door of the dwelling as possible.

When everyone is in the farthest room, stand in a circle and voice your intent for the ritual, saying something like:

*"We are gathered here to formally end our time
in this home. We will gather the good memories
and pack them within the flame of this candle.
We will cleanse the space with the scent and
smoke of this incense, so that this home may be
ready for its new life with new inhabitants."*

Light your candle and incense. Form a procession with the candle-bearer in front, followed by the incense-bearer. Last in line should be the "Closer," who is responsible for shutting out lights and closing doors behind the group. If you do not have people for each role, adjust accordingly.

Begin your procession by moving widdershins (counterclockwise) through the room. Shine the candle in every corner and follow with the incense, wafting smoke throughout the space. As you pass a window or door, close it. As you pass a light switch, turn it off. The Closer should be the last one out of the room, closing the door behind the ritual team.

As you move through the home, reminisce about good things you remember in each space as you pass through. What did you celebrate there? What is your fondest memory of a meal cooked in the kitchen? Of a guest who slept on your couch? Get your helpers to throw in some fun memories and share some laughs as you move from room to room.

Move in as close to a widdershins pattern as is possible throughout your home. Enter each room, hallway, and any closet large enough to step into, shining the candle and then censing with incense smoke.

As you carry the candle, visualize all the great moments you have celebrated in that space spiraling into the flame of the candle. Visualize the faces of people who have spent quality time in the home with you and the positive things you did together being packed up into the candlelight.

Just like any other process of packing to move, you can select what you want to take with you, and discard anything you want to get rid of. Do not pack anything into your candle that you don't want to keep.

Move from the highest point in the house to the lowest, covering the basement last. If you have any outbuildings that you have used in a significant way, you should consider processing through those as well.

When you have completed your widdershins pattern, and all the areas of your home have been "packed," censed, all the lights are turned off, and all doors and cupboards are closed, exit through the main door. Stand outside your former home, and thank it for the shelter it provided, and for the memories.

Use your candle snuffer to extinguish the flame. Visualize the positive things you have gathered being pushed into the candle and stored there. Carefully wrap your candle in cloth and store it safely until you move into your new home.

If the former home holds nothing but bad energy for you, gather any energy you don't want to leave behind, and store it in the candle. Wrap it in a black cloth and bury it. Alternately, if you have access to a place where you can have an outdoor fire, burn it.

Home Opening Ritual

When you arrive at your new home, choose a time when you can celebrate and hold a home opening ritual. This is essentially the same ritual as the home closing, but in reverse.

INGREDIENTS:

> The candle you closed your old home with
>
> Incense in a container that is safe to carry around (stick or loose incense work equally well)
>
> Household members or regular visitors to act as helpers
>
> Celebratory food and drink for after the ritual

Start by closing all the doors and windows and turning off all of the lights.

Walk into your new home through the main door. As soon as you are over the threshold, light your candle and incense. State your intent by saying something such as:

> *"We meet this home with love and peace in our hearts.*
> *May the sweet memories we bring be released, and*
> *may they be joined with many more good times and*
> *happy memories to come. May we take comfort and*
> *find peace here, with our family and friends!"*

Form your procession with the "Opener" in front to open all the doors and windows and to turn on all the lights. Next is the incense-bearer who will cense the space with the incense smoke, followed by the candle-bearer.

As you carry the candle, visualize the wonderful memories and energy from your old home being "unpacked" and pouring out of the candle, filling your new home with light.

Move in a deosil (clockwise) pattern around each room, turning on lights, opening doors, windows, and cupboards. Cense each area with the cleansing incense smoke and shine the candle in every nook and cranny. Try to move throughout the entire home in as close to a deosil pattern as possible. From the main door, move from the lowest point in the home to the highest (the basement to the attic). As you are moving through the new space, talk about your plans for your new home. Invite the rest of the team to add their hopes and dreams.

When you have opened the entire home up, and all the doors and windows are open, and all the lights on, leave your candle burning as you and your ritual team break out some food and drink to share. This feast doesn't have to be fancy. The customary moving-day pizza and beer will suffice, or whatever snacks and beverage you happen to have on hand.

Plant Magic—Making Medicine

To be able to source and create effective remedies in your own home is empowering and satisfying. I am including here two simple recipes using different techniques. You do not need to run out and buy anything special or expensive to be successful brewing them.

Infusions

Herbal infusions are a very practical way of extracting the nutritious and medicinal goodness from a plant, and easily consuming it. An infusion is essentially a tea, but you use more plant matter, and the steeping time is much longer. This process results in a darker, stronger drink. The longer steeping time allows the herb to release more of its medicinal properties. There is no hard and fast rule for the length of time to steep the herb; anywhere from thirty minutes to overnight may be necessary.

I make infusions using a 1-litre/1-quart glass jar, which gives me about four cups of the liquid to drink. If you find the infusion has an unpleasant taste, remember that it is good for you, and drink it anyway. You can add some honey to sweeten it up, and you might find that it is tastier to drink hot, cold, or at room temperature. Throwing some dried mint leaves in when you are making your infusion sometimes helps enhance the flavour.

Nettle Infusion

A favourite infusion of mine is made with stinging nettle, *Urtica dioica*. This remarkably nutritious plant can be found throughout most of the world and is often considered a weed. It is very common in North America, Europe, parts of Asia, and North Africa. It can be found growing along rivers and streams, in part-shade to full sun. It thrives in damp, nitrogen-rich soil. I like to wildcraft my nettle from the banks of the river that flows near my home. It is also commonly available at health food stores in dried form. If you have the space, it is worth transplanting some nettle into your garden.

Harvesting stinging nettle can be a delicate chore, as it earned its name for a reason—it does sting! The plant has tiny hairs along the leaves and stems which, when touched, break open to release a combination of chemicals that causes irritation to the skin. This is easy to get around by wearing long sleeves, and most importantly gloves, when you are harvesting the plant. If you do end up with a stinging rash, nature has provided a cure, which can usually be found growing in the same habitat as the nettles. Plantain or dock leaves can be crushed and applied as a poultice to the rash and will neutralize the sting. Calamine lotion is also handy to take the sting away.

Once harvested, nettle is easy to dry. Tie it in small, even bundles, and hang it in a cool dry place until it has completely dried out. Strip the dried leaves from any hard stems and store in a jar, away from direct sunlight.

Ingredients:

> A 1-litre/1-quart glass jar with lid
>
> 1 ounce of dried stinging nettle leaf
>
> Very hot water
>
> A fine-meshed sieve or cheesecloth

Place the dried nettle into your glass jar. Bring your water to a simmer. There is some debate about whether you should make infusions using boiling water. Some say that boiling water can destroy the delicate compounds in the plant matter, while others say it doesn't matter. My advice is to bring it to a simmer; it works, and you aren't taking the chance that you are damaging anything. Fill the jar halfway with water. This is when the dried nettle tends to float to the top, so take a moment to give it a good stir with something non-reactive, like a chopstick or the handle of a wooden spoon. Fill the jar up to the top with more water. Put the lid on the jar right away to keep the volatile compounds inside the jar. Let it sit for a minimum of four hours, but twelve hours works the best. I like to make it before I go to bed, so it is ready for me to drink when I get up in the morning.

When the infusion has finished steeping, strain it using a sieve. The spent nettle makes great compost, so don't toss it out if you can help it.

The infusion makes an earthy and curiously refreshing drink. I refer to it as "my swamp water" because of the murky green colour. It tastes best to me at room temperature, but it is also good cold. It lasts a couple days in the fridge, but once you make some, it really is best to drink it up on the same day.

Nettle infusion is an excellent pick-me-up. It is a rich with chlorophyll, high in vitamins, particularly A, C, and D, and it contains protein, calcium, iron, folate, potassium, magnesium, manganese, phosphorous, selenium, and zinc. The same infusion you make to drink can also be used as a hair rinse to enhance shine and treat dandruff.

I discovered nettle when I was dealing with adrenal fatigue. My local herbalist suggested I try nettle, and it gave me a sense of energy and well-being. It can also assist with insomnia, prevents allergies, and supports healthy urinary function.

Tinctures

Making tinctures is more involved than infusions, and they take a bit more work and investment. They also take longer to steep. The handy thing about them is that a tincture is a very compact way to preserve the medicinal goodness of a plant, and you can store it for a long time. Your best bet for storage is in those little coloured glass bottles that come with a built-in dropper. If you can't find those, any dark-coloured glass bottle with a tight-fitting lid will do. A small bottle of tincture is easy to take with you, and they can be either added to liquid to drink, or a dose of it can be placed directly under your tongue.

The making process is fun and pretty simple:

1. Select your menstruum. A menstruum is the liquid you will use. The most common is alcohol. Any cheap, 80-proof vodka is a good option. It has a fairly neutral flavour and it works. I have also experimented with rum and brandy. As long as you have something that is at least 80-proof (40 percent alcohol) and like the taste, it should work. Do NOT use rubbing alcohol; it is toxic! If alcohol is not an option for you, vinegar (apple cider vinegar has its own medicinal qualities to contribute) or food-grade vegetable glycerin can be substituted. The shelf-life of vinegar is shorter than alcohol, and glycerin is not as efficient at extracting the plants' chemical compounds.

2. Clean and sanitize a glass jar with hot water and soap. Rinse it well with hot water. A plastic lid works best if using vinegar, as metal can corrode.

3. Are you using fresh or dried herbs? Both will work, but fresh is better. Chop or tear them up and fill your jar with them.

4. Pour your menstruum into your jar of herbs, ensuring that you completely cover them. Use a chopstick or wooden spoon handle to stir out any bubbles.

5. Put the lid on your jar and store it away from direct sunlight. A dark closet or cupboard it best. If you can get amber coloured glass jars for this, that is optimal. Don't forget to put a label on it with the name of the plant and the date you made it.

6. Let your tincture steep for at least four weeks. Medicine-making like this is an excellent full moon activity. If you can acquire your herbs, either by harvesting or purchasing them, on a full moon and then make the tincture,

you know it will be ready to use by the time the next full moon comes around.

7. After at least one lunar cycle, strain your tincture. You can use a fine sieve, but I prefer a few layers of cheese-cloth. I like to pour my tincture out of the jar, through the cheesecloth, and into a large measuring cup, as it has a spout. This makes pouring my finished product into smaller stoppered bottles much easier.

8. Gently press the cheesecloth to wring out the last drops of tincture and add the spent plant matter to your compost pile, if you have one.

9. Whatever type of bottle you have to store your finished tincture in, do not forget to label it! I like to write any details about the moon phase it was created and bottled on the label, along with the name of the plant used and the date.

When you are starting out making tinctures, start small, one jar at a time. A 1-litre/1-quart glass jar produces a surprising amount of tincture, and you can always make another batch.

MOTHERWORT TINCTURE

A rewarding addition to your healing witch's apothecary is motherwort tincture. I adore this plant, so consider this my love letter to *Leonurus cardiaca*, motherwort. In 1653, herbalist Nicholas Culpeper wrote as accurate a tribute as you can find about this plant in his book *The Complete Herbal*: "There is no better herb to drive melancholy vapours from the heart, to strengthen it, and make the mind cheerful, blithe and merry."[6]

---

6   Nicholas Culpeper, *Culpeper's English Physician; and Complete Herbal* (London: E. Sibly, 1794), 253.

The common name of this plant can be attributed to its effectiveness at regulating menstrual cycles and calming menopause and PMS symptoms. It is a remedy often recommended by midwives for easing the stress of childbirth and treating postpartum depression. The medicinal properties of motherwort are helpful for everyone. Motherwort is used for insomnia, neuralgia, sciatica, spasms, fevers, and stomachaches.[7] I have personally used motherwort to treat my PMS and then menopause symptoms successfully. I also continue to use it for stress and anxiety.

Given all these benefits, it seems like a good thing that motherwort is such an invasive, persistent plant. As our society and culture continues to increase just about everyone's stress levels, it seems only fitting that motherwort is so abundant. Native to Europe and Asia, it was brought to North America by colonists as a healing herb and has aggressively spread far and wide. It loves to grow in neglected and liminal places, along roadways, riverbanks, woodlands, vacant lots, or just about anywhere. Usually reviled as a weed, it is not one you find being promoted at your garden centre.

Motherwort is a deep green perennial that grows up to five feet tall; it has a tough, square stem with three-lobed leaves. The calyx of the motherwort has five sharp points that resemble the five points of a pentagram, a nice thing for a witch to find when out wildcrafting! Remember to wear gloves when harvesting though, those points are sharp enough to pierce skin. Motherwort belongs to the mint family, but unlike most familiar mints, it lacks the sweet "minty" flavour and tends to be rather bitter. It blooms pink to lavender coloured tubular flowers in the early summer, and this is the best time to harvest it. Use pruning shears to take the top

---

7   Steven Foster and James A. Duke, *A Field Guide to Medicinal Plants and Herbs of Eastern and Central North America, 2nd. ed.* (New York: Houghton Mifflin, 2000), 182.

third of each plant, including the stem, leaves, and flowers. This is what you will use to make your tincture.

Chop up your motherwort, put it in your jar, fill with your chosen menstruum, and let it rest a moon cycle in a dark place. When it is ready it will be very bitter and dark.

DOSE: ½–1½ teaspoon, three times per day.

If you have excessively heavy bleeding during your menstrual cycles, this is not for you. The calming and "ability to cope" effect of motherwort can also become addictive, so be aware of your limits.

One cold and wet evening I got a phone call from one of my Intro to Witchcraft students. She was extremely concerned about one of her friends who had delivered a baby the day before, after a particularly difficult and dramatic labour. The new mother had the assistance of a midwife and had hoped for a home birth, but because of many complications, the mother was rushed to a hospital. The babe arrived safe and perfect, but the mother was really stressed and suffering, and they had already been discharged from the hospital. It was fairly late in the evening, and the midwife could not locate any motherwort tincture to help the new mom. Upon hearing this, my student phoned me and asked if I had any motherwort tincture that I could spare. Well, of course I did, and as luck would have it, the mother and baby were within walking distance of my home. So, I bundled up, grabbed an umbrella, and headed over to deliver the goods. I felt every inch the village witch as I slogged through the puddles and braced against the wind. How many times has this plant been called to help in such a situation? Knocking on the door, I was greeting by a very concerned and sleep-deprived new father, who thanked me up and down for the gift. It was a great day to be a witch.

Black Salt—to Defend, Absorb, and Protect

The black salt used in magic can be either purchased in your local occult shop or purchased online, but if you want to be in control of how it is made and the ingredients that go into it, making it yourself ensures that you will get what you want. There are many recipes out there for creating black salt and you can make it as simple or elaborate as you like. Your own tradition or magical path may have a tried-and-true method for making and using black salt, so it is worth doing your own research, and experimenting to find out what is most effective for you.

If you are dealing with a situation where you feel that you are under some form of attack, making some black salt is a relatively simple way to get some control over the situation.

Ingredients:
 A mortar and pestle
 White salt of your choice

Place the blackening ingredient of your choice, or combination thereof, into your mortar. Some common options are:
 Charcoal from a wood fire
 Activated charcoal (available at health food stores)
 Charcoal brick (the kind you burn loose incense on)
 Black pepper
 Iron filings from a cast iron pan or cauldron

Note: some black salt is made using food dyes. This is effective for getting a rich dark colour, but you will have to decide how you feel about chemical additives in your finished product.

Using your pestle, grind up the blackening ingredients into a powder. Slowly add your salt, mixing well until you have an even texture, and the salt is well mixed and coloured black. Store this in an airtight container until you are ready to use it.

To take your black salt to another level, you can add the ash of burnt herbs that are relevant to the type of magical defense you need. A comprehensive herbal book is very helpful for learning the magical associations of herbs, starting with the ones you have in your kitchen.

Gather one or more of the herbs you want, burn them in a fireproof dish, and then add the ashes to your salt mixture. Some options are:

Basil: attracts benevolent spirits, promotes courage

Burdock root: protection for the home

Rue: protection from evil eye, nightmares, evil spirits; also helps safeguard the traveller on astral journeys

Sage: protection for the astral body while journeying

Valerian: protection from evil sorcery; helps counter negative magic

You can boost your black salt by adding a couple of drops of essential oil to the mix.

Cinnamon: for protection from toxic romantic relationships

Clove: for protection and courage; wards off jealousy

Juniper: for enforcing boundaries; protection from malevolent witchcraft and evil entities

Lavender: for psychic protection

Pine: dispels negative energy and is particularly helpful to cleanse sacred space and objects

White Salt—To Cleanse Your Space

INGREDIENTS:

    a small bowl that you like the look of

    enough white salt to fill the bowl almost to the top

Place your bowl on your working altar, preferably on your pentacle. In a pinch, or if you are doing this work somewhere other than your home, you can improvise by drawing a pentacle on a piece of paper while visualizing your intent.

Pour the salt into the bowl. Speak your intent to the Spirits of Salt by saying something like: "Spirits of Salt, I call on you to aid and assist with the cleansing of this space." I encourage you to say this out loud. The impact of your words will be felt not only by the spirits you wish to connect with, but the sound of your words in our own ears will have a profound effect on you as well.

When your salt bowl is ready, place it in a safe but conspicuous place in your space. Leave it there for three days. At the end of the third day, safely dispose of the salt, and refill the bowl. Repeat this again in three more days. After you have completed this three times three-day cycle, you should be able to feel that the atmosphere has become lighter in your space. If you feel more intense scrubbing is required, try starting on the new moon and changing the salt every three days until the full moon.

Once you are satisfied with your results, you may consider maintaining a salt bowl as part of your regular routine, changing it every month at the new moon.

Chapter 12

THE EARTH WHEEL OF THE YEAR AND WITCHIN' IN THE KITCHEN

The most basic expression of the element of earth at a celebration is food. Gathering with your nearest and dearest to share food and each other's company is a form of celebration as old as humanity. This comes from the basic human need to gather, feast, and acknowledge special times with some form of ritual. We are sharing the bounty of Mother Earth, and the sacrifice of her plants and animals. Sometimes we say prayers, give toasts, or make speeches at such meals. These simple rituals are embedded in all cultures because they are effective, and they nourish not only our physical bodies, but our spirits as well.

When I get together with my spiritual family for a meal, we always start off with a blessing for the feast. Taking the time to ritually acknowledge the abundance we are about to share imparts a sense of the sacred into the occasion and gives us an opportunity to savour the preciousness of our food and the efforts of all involved in its creation. I wrote these words years ago, and hearing them repeated grounds and centres into the moment, reminding us of all the great feasts we have shared, family and friends, old and new:

Boreal Heart Coven Food Blessing

In the name of the Silver Lady of the Night Sky,

And the Horned Lord of the Wild Places,

We bless this feast.

Food is the product of all of the elements

working together in perfect love and perfect trust,

to nurture and sustain us.

We are grateful for this feast,

and all of the hands,

both seen and unseen,

who have brought it here to feed us.

Blessed be.

When I lived alone with my beloved dog and cat, we had our own feasting ritual. Every second Friday was payday, and on my way home from work I would either pick up some sushi or a rotisserie chicken. If it was a chicken night, I would share with my dog (my cat wasn't into it). On a sushi night the cat would get a little bit of raw fish. No matter what I was eating, special pet treats would also be liberally shared with both of my companions. After a big dose of catnip for Roddy the Cat, my dog Oban and I would head out for a walk. This is how we celebrated payday. It was our little weird family's simple yet meaningful food ritual.

In my Witchcraft practice, I celebrate the wheel of the year with my coven. Depending on the sabbat, we may invite other Pagan folk and sometimes our non-Pagan family to join in the festivities. There is always food and ritual. These two things are universal enough so that even if the attendees are from different paths, everyone can agree that the rituals add form and foundation to the season, and that the food is always abundant and delicious.

Food is also part of our rituals. In Wiccan traditions, the "cakes and ale" part of the ceremony is when food and drink is ritually consecrated and then shared amongst the participants. This bestows the blessings of the deities and has the extra benefit of helping the participants ground themselves after the magical working and energy raising that is usually performed before the cakes and ale are served. Eating something helps us to ground because it reconnects us to the most basic needs of our body and brings us back to the physical and present moment.

Sabbat Celebrations and Witchin' in the Kitchen

I love preparing and sharing food and drink for my nearest and dearest folks. Nothing is more satisfying to me than knowing that the people closest to me are well fed and content. Celebrating the festivals on the Witch's Wheel of the Year provides eight great opportunities to gather, celebrate, and practice some kitchen witchery.

To be a kitchen witch is to reframe your perspective on your kitchen and the food you prepare in it. You must look at your kitchen as a kind of temple, and the food you prepare in it as a sacred offering of health, comfort, hospitality, and generosity. It is about not taking anything for granted, gratitude for the sacrifice of the plants and animals that are your food, and a mindfulness to not be wasteful or frivolous with resources.

In my kitchen I try to remember to reflect the ethos I want to see in the world. I compost and recycle. I prioritize fresh, local, and homemade food as much as I possibly can. I like to experiment with new recipes and learn from the cuisines of other cultures. I love to collect herbs and spices and research for inventive ways to use them. When I travel, I like to check out food stores for interesting foodstuffs to bring home and try out for myself. My "Cookbook of Shadows" is a big three-ring binder stuffed with recipes I have collected, invented, or been given by friends, and I add my own notes about the things I have made, and noted where I have added or changed things to suit my tastes. This is fun to look back on, like a culinary scrapbook of creativity and exploration.

Years ago, when I started to learn about witchcraft, my mentor gave me a list of correspondences that included the types of food associated with each sabbat and element. Since then, I have come across other such lists and they are all pretty similar. Foods that are associated with earth are typically hearty and comforting. Crops that grow underground, such as root vegetables like carrots, parsnips, and beets, or tubers such as potatoes or yams, are hearty earthy fare. Foods that hug the ground on bushes or vines such as summer squashes or winter squashes like pumpkin, zucchini, or acorn squash are also associated with earth. The meat from earth-associated animals like beef, goat, and pork would also be considered earth foods and so are most seeds and nuts. We all have foods that we consider "comfort foods" or favorite recipes that make us feel homey and cozy and these may be your personal earth foods or dishes.

I will argue that foods preserved and stored using traditional methods such as canning, salting, or fermentation should be considered earth element foods. I am a dedicated food preserver, and I can attest to the earthy satisfaction of opening a jar of home canned tomatoes from the summer to make hot, warming soup in the winter. Fermenting vegetables using nothing but salt and the natural juices of the veggies and watching them bubble and transform into an even more nutrient-rich delicacy is earth magic manifest in the kitchen!

Samhain

Often regarded as the Witch's New Year, Samhain is a time to honour the dead, and do some spiritual reflection and clearing out. This festival marks the third and final harvest of the year, when the last of the crops are brought in and the reality of winter is right on our doorstep. Many Witchcraft traditions believe that at Samhain the veil that separates our world from the realm of the dead is very thin, and that this is an optimum time for communication with our Beloved and Mighty Dead—the Beloved being our personal ancestors, such as family or close friends and people whom we had personal relationships with; and the Mighty Dead being deceased magical practitioners who have kept the Craft alive and left behind a body of knowledge that we can benefit and learn from. Magically this is also a good time of year to do banishing magic, divination, and psychopomp work.

Pumpkin Pie

In the autumn of 2004, I was living in the small village of Meare, just outside of Glastonbury, England. As Samhain approached, I decided that I would make pumpkin pie for the sabbat feast my Witchcraft group was planning. Growing up in Canada, pumpkin pie is mandatory at this time of year and I really can't imagine autumn without it—it's a comfort-of-home type thing. I headed to Tesco's to pick some up. No luck. I hit every grocery store within driving distance and no pumpkin. Every shop clerk I asked thought I was insane (who puts a pumpkin in a can?) and said they had never heard of such a thing. I had no idea that it was such a North American-specific food. Finally, the nice man who ran the village shop in Meare (who also shook his head at me) gave me a pumpkin saying, "If you manage to turn this into a pie, I want some." It was a big jack-o-lantern type pumpkin, not a pie pumpkin, but I took it home and roasted it to make puree for pie filing anyway. It was a bit watery, but when the spices were added and the pie was baked, it looked good and tasted like a slice of home. My friends were skeptical but ate some anyway. Most of them liked it and were surprised it was sweet. The guy at the village shop laughed when I walked in with his slice. He carefully ate it, not believing it was made of the same pumpkin he had given me. Since then, "pumpkin spice everything" has taken over, and I can't help but wonder if you can now get canned pumpkin in the UK. I have honed my recipe over the years, so here it is...

INGREDIENTS:

- 1 pastry for single-crust pie (store bought or homemade, both work fine)
- 1–398 ml can of pumpkin puree (about 1¾ cups)
- 1 cup of evaporated milk
- 2 large eggs PLUS 2 extra egg yolks
- ¾ cup light brown sugar
- ⅓ cup sour cream
- 1 teaspoon vanilla extract
- 1½ teaspoon cinnamon
- ½ teaspoon nutmeg
- ⅛ teaspoon ground cloves
- 1 teaspoon ginger puree (the kind that comes in a jar, OR fresh grated OR ginger powder)
- ½ teaspoon salt

Preheat oven to 425°F.

Roll out the pastry and lay it into a 9" pie dish.

In a large bowl, lightly beat the eggs and extra egg yolks. Add in the pumpkin, evaporated milk, and sour cream and whisk until blended. Add in the sugar, vanilla, spices, and salt.

When everything is well mixed, pour it carefully into the pie shell. Place it in the oven and let it bake for 15 minutes, then reduce the temperature to 375°F for an additional 40–45 minutes. The centre of the pie filling should just jiggle a little bit if you nudge it, and the crust should be golden brown. Let it cool on the counter for a couple hours. The pie will continue to set as it cools. Serve at room temperature, or chilled, with a dollop of whipped cream.

Winter Solstice

This sabbat is also called Yule and is usually celebrated sometime around December 20. Many Neopagans celebrate by staying up all through the longest night, sitting vigil and awaiting the return of the sun. In some Wiccan traditions the story of the battle between the Oak King and Holly King marks the season. The Holly King is challenged by the Oak King to fight, with the Oak King winning control of the next half of the year as the daylight lengthens. The feasting that happens at this time of year is a welcome break from the long cold nights where I live, and it is such a treat to have the company of loved ones around to celebrate the solstice. As the light grows, this is an effective time to do magic related to manifesting what you want or need in your life and setting goals for yourself.

Stuffed Acorn Squash

This dish makes a hearty meal for two; just add some salad or other veggies on the side, or if you cut the baked acorn squash halves into quarters, you have a nice side dish to go along with roast meat. You can change up the flavour by using other types of cheese or herbs and chopped bits of apple, or bits of dried fruit give it a "turkey stuffing" vibe. This is a good one to serve at Yule or Christmas gatherings for guests who don't eat meat and it can easily be adapted for vegans as well.

Ingredients:

    1 acorn squash

    ½ cup uncooked quinoa

    ½ of a medium onion, diced small

    6 large mushrooms, diced

    1 heaping tablespoon each of raw sunflower seed and pumpkin seed

    1 teaspoon rubbed sage

    1 teaspoon dried thyme

    ½ teaspoon dried rosemary, crushed

    Salt and pepper to taste

    1 cup grated cheddar cheese plus extra for topping

    Generous handful chopped fresh parsley

Preheat oven to 375°F.

Cut the acorn squash in half from stem to tip and scoop out all the seeds. Lay the halves bowl side up on a cookie sheet and rub all the cut surfaces with olive oil and season with salt and pepper. Roast in the oven for about 20 minutes, or until just tender when poked with a fork.

While the squash is roasting, prepare your stuffing. Cook the quinoa according to package directions. Chop up the onions and sauté them in a pan gently until they start turning golden brown, and then add the chopped mushrooms. As the mushrooms release their juices, add the dried herbs and seeds. Season with salt and pepper. Add in parsley, stir until wilted, and remove pan from heat.

Combine the cooked quinoa, sautéed vegetables, and cheese in a bowl and mix well. Taste it and adjust seasoning as needed. When the squash is just tender, remove from oven. Scoop the stuffing into the hollows of the squash halves and pack it down. You will have enough stuffing to create a generous pile on each half, so pat it down so that it covers the squash and looks nice. Sprinkle some extra cheese on top and put the squash back into the oven for about 20 minutes, until the cheese is melted and golden.

Brown rice can be substituted for quinoa, but it doesn't quite stick to the squash the same way. I have also made this using crumbled sausage meat in the filling, which is very hearty and delicious.

Imbolc

The sabbat of Imbolc (sometimes spelled Imbolg) falls on or about February 2 and has its roots in the pre-Christian traditions of Celtic cultures. Historically this holiday is connected to the goddess Brigid, a goddess of healing, smithcraft, and poetry. It is also sometimes conflated with the Christian festival of Candlemas, which occurs on February 2 and commemorates the Virgin Mary presenting her son Jesus to the temple in Jerusalem forty days after his birth. Folklore from Ireland links this time of year with the lactation of sheep, the birthing of lambs, and the offering of butter. These references to dairy products and the returning of fertility to livestock don't translate well to modern urban life, but they are in keeping with the spirit of the next recipe.

Homemade Yogurt

I got myself into the routine of making yogurt at home years ago and now I can't imagine buying premade yogurt at the store. Homemade yogurt is cheap and easy to make once you learn a couple of tricks. It is tangy and some may say a little bit sour compared to the sugar-infused commercial stuff, but you will get to control what you add to it before you eat it.

The key is to start with the best milk you can afford. Organic, whole milk is ideal. You can use skim, 1%, or 2%, but they will produce a runnier yogurt. The fat in whole milk gives your final product more body and flavour. The second thing you will need is some plain, natural yogurt to act as your starter. For this check out the organic dairy section at the grocery store and look for one that lists "live active cultures" in the ingredients. Do not try to use anything with any flavourings or sweeteners added, as these will cause your yogurt to fail.

EQUIPMENT:
Large heavy-bottomed pot
2 x 1-litre (quart) jars with lids
1/2 cup sized jar with lid
Thermometer (optional, but handy)
Oven, with interior light

INGREDIENTS:
2 litres (2 quarts) of whole organic milk
½ cup of natural organic yogurt

Start by turning your oven on to the lowest temperature, which for most models will be somewhere around 170°F. When the oven reaches temperature, turn the heat OFF and turn the oven light ON.

Meanwhile, pour your milk into a large, heavy-bottomed pot and set it on a stovetop element at a medium-high setting. Heat the milk to about 82°C (185°F). If you don't have a thermometer, you will know it has reached temperature when it starts to steam and form bubbles on the surface. This process kills off any unwanted bacteria that may be lurking in your milk. Do not let it boil and do not scrape the bottom of the pot if you stir it. The bottom may scorch a bit and scraping the bottom may leave a burnt taste in the yogurt.

Remove the bubbling, steaming pot from the stove and set it aside to cool down. You want the temperature of the milk to go down to around 45°C (115°F). You can judge this without a thermometer by testing it with your finger—you should be able to hold your finger in it for five seconds comfortably. If it is too hot you will kill your starter culture and if it is just right, your starter culture will go to work on your milk, converting it to yogurt.

Place your starter yogurt in a small bowl and add about a cup of warm milk, stirring it smooth. Pour this mixture into your milk and give it a good stir. Transfer your milk mixture into two clean 1-litre jars and your small jar. The small jar will be your starter for your next batch of yogurt.

Place all three jars in your warm oven with the light on. The light will give just enough ambient warmth to maintain a good temperature for your yogurt to incubate in.

Let the yogurt sit for at least eight hours. I usually prepare this in the evening and let it incubate overnight. In the morning pull the jars out of the oven and let them stand on the counter for a bit before tucking them in the fridge. The yogurt will finish setting in the fridge and will be best to eat when it gets a chance to chill.

Spoon some yogurt in a bowl and top it with whatever you like. Granola, frozen berries, fresh fruit—it's up to you! Maple syrup or honey are great sweeteners.

Spring Equinox

The sabbat celebrated as winter gives way to the spring is also called Ostara. In the Northern Hemisphere, this is the time when the daylight hours regain their strength, and the land wakes up from its slumber. This is a time of youth, vitality, and sowing seeds, actually and metaphorically. What do you want to manifest this year? What do you want to grow?

If we were all truly agricultural people, we would be existing off the last of our preserved food stores by now and craving the freshness of a green and growing garden or freshly foraged foods. This recipe celebrates the glow of a hardy root crop seasoned with a hint of spice to take the chill out.

Root Soup

Spring Equinox in my part of the world can be really, really cold. Hot warming soup that is the colour of the sun is good medicine for a chilly day. Carrots are reliably available all year long and they keep well in the fridge. Parsnips add their earthy flavour and a touch of natural creaminess. A farmer friend turned me on to parsley root and when I added it to this recipe it made it really special. I don't see it in the stores near me, but if you find some, try adding it in.

INGREDIENTS:

    3 cups peeled and diced carrots

    2 cups peeled and diced parsnips

    1 medium-sized cooking onion peeled and diced

    2 Tbsp grated ginger root

    3 cloves garlic, crushed and diced

    1 400 ml can of coconut milk

    2 cups vegetable stock (homemade, store bought, or from a bouillon cube, does not matter)

    3 Tbsp butter

    Salt and pepper, to taste

Peel and chop all your vegetables.

Over medium-high heat melt butter in a heavy pot and add the onions and sauté until they are tender. Add carrots and parsnips and continue to sauté until they get soft.

Add the ginger and garlic and stir well. Continue to cook for 2–3 minutes.

Add the can of coconut milk and then stir in the stock. Let the soup simmer gently until the vegetables are very tender.

Remove from heat and then, using an immersion blender, puree the soup until it is well blended and creamy. You can also transfer the hot soup into a blender to puree or, in a pinch, mash with a potato masher to make it as smooth as possible. Add a bit of water or broth to thin it out if necessary.

Season with salt and pepper and serve.

Note: If you want to change this up a bit, add a tablespoon of curry powder when you add the garlic and ginger. It is also delicious to drizzle sesame oil on the top of each bowl and garnish with chopped cilantro.

You can make this soup with any combination of carrots, parsnips, and parsley root, if you can find it. The point is to have about five cups of root veggies for the soup. Even just plain carrot is delicious. Changing the vegetable stock for chicken stock, or the coconut milk for cream, can add variety to this simple recipe. I sometimes throw in a teaspoon of cumin and a pinch of cinnamon, depending on my mood.

Beltane

The festival of Beltane falls between the spring equinox and the Summer Solstice. It is a celebration of fertility and the emergence of new life and fecundity. Typical Neopagan celebrations tend to include outdoor celebrations, bonfires, and dancing the maypole.

It is often regarded as a romantic time of year, with weddings and handfastings being celebrated and love blooming.

This sabbat sits opposite Samhain on the Wheel of the Year, and it is also considered a time when the veil between the worlds is thin. If we honour our dead at Samhain, it seems fitting to honour the reborn at Beltane. Contemporary Neopagan Beltane celebrations tend to fixate on the male/female polarity aspect, and this does not necessarily resonate with everyone. If the birth/death/rebirth cycle is to be celebrated fairly, Beltane provides a sabbat for also welcoming back the reincarnated souls to this world.

Curry Stuffed Eggs

Eggs are a universal symbol of fertility, birth, and resurrection. They hold the promise of life and the mystery of creation. Myths from ancient civilizations of India, Egypt, and Greece speak of the world being created from a great cosmic egg. In Asian cultures eggs are symbols of material wealth and luck.

They are also very tasty, and stuffed eggs make great picnic food. These eggs can be prepped in advance and taken along to celebrate the promise of spring.

INGREDIENTS:

6 large eggs

¼ cup mayonnaise

1 tsp Dijon mustard

1 tsp curry powder

Salt and fresh ground pepper, to taste

Cayenne pepper to garnish

Chopped chives, to garnish

Start by making hard-boiled eggs. Place your eggs in the bottom of a pot so that they are not crowded, and fill with enough water to cover them by at least an inch. Place the pot on the stove and with the element on high, bring the water to a rolling boil. Turn off the element, put a lid on the pot, and leave it on the burner for 10–12 minutes. Lift the eggs out of the hot water and transfer to a bowl of ice water to cool down completely. You can prep your eggs as much as five days in advance as hard-boiled eggs keep very well in the fridge.

Peel the eggs and then slice them in half lengthwise. Carefully scoop out the yolks and place them in a bowl. Set aside the whites on a serving platter. I like to lay them on some salad greens to prop them up.

Add the mayonnaise, mustard, curry powder, salt, and pepper to the egg yolks and mash them together until the mixture is very smooth and creamy.

Spoon the curried yolk mixture into the "cups" of the whites. If you want to be fancy, transfer the curried mixture into a zip top bag and then cut the tip of one of the corners off to make a piping bag and pipe it into the egg whites. Garnish with sprinkles of cayenne pepper and chives. Serve slightly chilled.

Summer Solstice

This summer sabbat is sometimes called Midsummer or Litha. This is usually a great time to take celebrations outdoors for a bonfire, raucous merrymaking, and basking in the glow of your accomplishments. Now we see the return of the battle between the Oak King and the Holly King. This time it is the Holly King who defeats his rival and takes control as the days grow shorter leading up to the winter solstice.

Peach Jam

Fresh peaches are the flavour of summer. They don't grow where I live; our winters are too cold for the trees. I do get a little delirious with glee when baskets of peaches start showing up in the grocery stores and fruit stands around my hometown, trucked in from the Okanagan Valley of British Columbia or southern Ontario.

If you have never tried canning before, this is an easy first project that tastes great and feels kind of fancy. Do not be intimidated by the idea of canning your own food. This is a great skill to develop and really comes in handy, especially if you have a garden, or for when you come across deals on fresh produce. Putting up jars of your own canned food and saving it for later is, to me, one of the earthiest things to do in the kitchen. I am extremely grateful to eat last summer's tomatoes in the heart of January or savour the sweetness of berries I picked and turned into jam last July. The sight of a cupboard stocked with jars of food I preserved myself gives me peace of mind, and the beautiful colours shining through the glass look like precious gems.

I am not crazy about overly sweet preserves. The way I was taught to make jam called for a frightening amount of sugar and I was never happy with the results. Then I noticed a low-sugar pectin in a health food store one day, and making jam and jelly became really rewarding. It is worth it to search out a low-sugar pectin, and brands like Pomona or Bernardin are quite popular in North America and can be ordered online if you need to. They allow you to reduce the sugar or skip it entirely and use honey or whatever sweetener you prefer instead.

This recipe will yield about five cups of jam. To can the jam, you will need five 250 ml (approx. 8 oz) jars with appropriate snap lids and screw bands. You will also need a big pot to process your filled jars in. Canning pots come with a special rack to support the jars, but if you don't have one, any big pot with enough space to comfortably hold the jars in an upright position with enough water to cover them with about two inches of water will also work. If you don't have a rack, you must put something in the bottom of your pot, or your jars will crack. A folded tea towel will work in a pinch, or a cooling rack that you would use for baking. I once even used a metal vegetable steaming basket.

To sterilize your jars, place them in your canning pot filled with enough water to submerge and cover them by at least two inches. Boil them for at least 10 minutes. Prepare your snap lids by putting them in a small pot and boiling them for 5 minutes and then leaving them in the warm water until you are ready to can the jam.

If you decide not to can this jam, just pour it into jars and let it cool and then stick it in the fridge.

INGREDIENTS:

- 4 cups of peeled, chopped, and mashed peaches
- ¼ cup bottled lemon juice
- ¾ cup of honey
- ½ teaspoon almond extract (not essential, but it adds a wonderful depth of flavour)
- 3 teaspoons Pomona pectin powder
- 4 teaspoons calcium water (this comes with the pectin)

Sterilize your canning jars and set aside. Boil your snap lids and have them ready to go in the warm water.

Peel your peaches and chop them up, mashing them slightly as you go. Measure 4 cups of the mashed fruit and add it to a saucepan along with the bottled lemon juice and almond extract.

Follow the package directions on the pectin box to prepare the calcium water. Do not skip this step as the calcium activates the pectin and is necessary for the jam to set.

Add the 4 teaspoons of prepared calcium water to the mashed peaches in the saucepan and stir it thoroughly.

Measure the honey and place it in a bowl. Add the pectin powder to the honey and stir it until the pectin powder has been mixed in very well and set aside.

Bring the peach mixture to a boil and stir in the honey mixture. Stir it for two minutes so that everything combines and the pectin dissolves.

Bring everything to a boil and then remove the pot from stove. Fill your jars to about ¼ inch from the top. Wipe the lip of the jars to remove any drips with a clean damp cloth. Place the snap lids on the jar and secure them with a screw band.

Using tongs or a jar lifter, lower your sealed jars into the canning pot and bring to a boil and process for 10 minutes (add an extra minute for every 1,000 feet above sea level). Remove your jars carefully when they are done and let them rest on the counter for 24 hours. Check to make sure that the lids have "snapped" down. They are properly sealed if they curve downward.

Open a jar of summer in the depths of winter and savour the sweetness.

Lughnasadh

This cross-quarter sabbat falls between the blazing glory of Summer Solstice and the liminal Autumn Equinox, on or about August 1. Lughnasadh (pronounced LOO-nah-sah) is linked with the Celtic god Lugh and translates to "the marriage of Lugh." The sabbat celebrates the union of Lugh, a solar-associated deity, with the Earth Mother, or the land. Together they create the fertility of the crops, and this is the time of the first harvest.

Some Pagans use the name Lammas interchangeably with Lughnasadh, but they are different celebrations with similar spirit. Lammas (loaf-mass) is an early Christian observance celebrated on August 1, when grain from the first harvest was baked into bread and then consecrated during mass.

Harvesting and sharing the first foods of the harvest is a great way to celebrate this sabbat. This is a great time of year to make mead. I am lucky to live in a part of the world where lots of folks, in the city and in the country, have really embraced beekeeping. By the time Lughnasadh rolls around, fresh, local honey is available and affordable. As flying insects, bees may seem to be a creature of air, but their important role in agriculture and pollination, coupled with their orderly and structured hive colonies, connect them firmly to earth.

Blessed Bee Mead

As the main ingredient in mead, honey is the star of the show. It is absolutely worth paying a bit extra and taking the time to find the very best unpasteurized, natural honey that you can afford. Honey provides the character and flavour for the mead, so if you like the way the honey tastes, you will love the way the mead tastes after your care and effort has been put into making it into mead.

The water you use will also influence your final product. Use the purest water you can get your hands on. This is one occasion when I sometimes break down and purchase spring water from a store, and you may want to do this if your own tap water has a high mineral content or a high chemical load. At very least, boil enough water plus some the day before you make the mead, and let it stand uncovered overnight. This will at least get rid of some chemicals.

INGREDIENTS:

    1 quart plain natural honey

    1 gallon water (plus some extra)

    1 package champagne yeast (Lalvin EC 1118 works well)

EQUIPMENT:

    Large stockpot

    2 x 1-gallon glass jugs

    1 airlock with rubber bung that fits the mouth of the jug

    1 siphon hose

    7 (at least) 500 ml flip-top Grolsch-style bottles

Make sure all your equipment and bottles are very clean and sterilized.

Place your water and honey into the stockpot, and heat until it is steaming. You DO NOT want to boil this, as this will kill the honey aroma and flavour of the finished mead. Just get it steaming hot and keep it at this temperature for about two hours. Foam will rise to the top of your water/honey mixture, skim it off and discard.

After the liquid has simmered and the foam has stopped rising, remove the pot carefully from the heat, and let it stand until it cools down to a lukewarm temperature (no warmer than 25°C or 80°F). While you are waiting, activate the yeast by mixing it with about a cup of lukewarm water in a small bowl. Stir it to break up any lumps, and then cover it until the honey and water mixture cools down.

When your honey water is cool enough, siphon it into your gallon jug, and carefully add the yeast mixture. The liquid should come up the shoulder of the jug. If it is low (and it may be depending on how much you lost to evaporation) top it up with lukewarm extra water.

At this point I like to give it a good stir using the long handle of a wooden spoon. Prepare your airlock by filling it as indicated with water and fit it in the mouth of your jug.

Place your jug in a safe spot where it can be undisturbed, but you can keep an eye on it. It should be warm, but NOT hot. Leave it to ferment for about 7–21 days and watch the airlock. It will bubble as the mead releases gases. It will eventually slow down to about one bubble per minute and this tells you that this primary fermentation stage is about done.

Very carefully siphon your mead into your second clean 1-gallon jug, leaving behind any sediment. Clean and replace your airlock. Let this sit until it is clear, which takes anywhere from 1–4 months.

Now you can bottle! I use 500 ml flip top "Grolsch" bottles. They are handy because they have a built in "cork" that is reusable. Siphon your mead into the bottles, seal, and let rest for at least 6 months. It is ready to drink when you like the taste. Mead mellows over time, so if you taste it when you are siphoning and it is a bit raunchy, let it age, and the flavour will get better.

When I started making mead, I made my first batch based on a recipe for a spiced mead and worked backward from there, removing all the extra stuff until I had this recipe for plain mead. If you make a batch at Lughnasadh, you will have a nicely aged mead for Beltane … if you can stay out of it long enough!

Autumn Equinox

I must admit; this is my favourite sabbat. I love it. The autumn equinox usually falls somewhere around September 20–22, and it is that liminal time of year that teeters between the rich golden and russet colours of autumn and the long dark nights of winter, where I live, anyway. This sabbat is known by many names—Harvest Home, Harvesttide, Alban Elfed, and Mabon. Of this list, the name Mabon sparks the most controversy as it the most recent of the sabbat's names. In 1974, writer Aiden Kelly dubbed this holiday Mabon in a calendar he created. This usage was published in *Green Egg Magazine* and it stuck, becoming so popular that Neopagans embraced it as firmly as the more historically established names.

This is the second harvest festival, a time to gather in crops and put food away for the winter. Magically it is a good time to begin a period of reflection and dealing with any shadow work that you may have been putting off. Assess the material aspects of your magical practice—do you need any candles, herbs, or magical supplies for the coming season?

Fermented Sauerkraut

I LOVE fermenting foods. The magical alchemy of salt and fresh vegetables transforming into a tangy, tasty, nutritious fermented delicacy is so satisfying to make, and I find the process meditative and very satisfying. It just doesn't feel like home without something bubbling away on the kitchen counter. This simple recipe really shows off the power of salt to transform and preserve food.

The salt you use is the first factor in your success. You must use a natural salt, free of iodine and additives. For ferments, I prefer Celtic sea salt. It may be a bit pricey, but it is reliable and consistent. The salt will ensure your sauerkraut retains a nice crisp texture and will facilitate the lactobacillus bacteria that provides the delicious taste and health benefits in fermented food.

The water content in your cabbage will also be a factor in your result. A nice fresh, juicy cabbage will release more water when the salt is worked into it, creating more brine. This is optimal, but if your cabbage is on the dry side, have some pure water handy to add in if necessary.

INGREDIENTS:
    1 head of green cabbage (about 2 lbs)
    4 teaspoons of Celtic sea salt (or other natural salt NOT iodized table salt)

EQUIPMENT:
    Sharp knife
    Large mixing bowl
    1-litre/1-quart mason jar with a lid
    OR
    Fermentation lid with airlock
    Glass weight or small Ziploc bag

Remove any bruised or grubby-looking exterior leaves from the cabbage. Cut it in half lengthwise and cut out the tough core.

Using your sharp knife, or if you have one, a mandoline, slice the cabbage very thinly, about 3 mm or an eighth of an inch is perfect.

Put all your sliced cabbage in a big mixing bowl, and begin to knead it, as you would dough. As you work, sprinkle in the salt, one teaspoonful at a time.

The cabbage will start to break down and release its juices—this will form your brine. Leave it to stand for about 30 minutes. Check to make sure it is releasing water and give it a few extra squeezes along the way; you want your cabbage to go limp.

Pack the limp cabbage into your jar as firmly as you can. I use a muddler for this, but a wooden spoon works too. When your cabbage is all packed in, make sure you pour in any of the salty brine remaining in the bowl. Your brine needs to submerge your cabbage; this will make sure that your sauerkraut doesn't go bad. If it doesn't, add just enough pure water to cover the cabbage.

Here is where a glass weight comes in handy. It gets dropped in on top of the cabbage to hold it underwater. If you don't have one, use a small Ziploc bag with some water in it, and rest that on top of the cabbage. The Ziploc should be small enough to sit inside the jar, with just enough water in it (and the air squeezed out) to hold down the cabbage. If you don't have either—no worries. Just ensure your liquid is covering the cabbage and keep an eye out for any mould.

Screw on your lid. If you can find one with an airlock, it is helpful to have, but not essential. If you are using a regular lid, you will need to "burp" your sauerkraut daily as it ferments, to release the gases that are going to bubble up in there. Please do this! A build-up of gas can cause the jar to explode.

Let your sauerkraut sit on your counter in a spot where you can keep an eye on it, away from direct sunlight. It should start to bubble in 1–3 days or so, depending on the temperature in your kitchen. Taste it after about three weeks. If it isn't sour enough for you, just let it sit longer. Once it has a flavour you like, remove the weights and move it to the fridge. It will keep for quite a long time, provided you keep the cabbage covered in brine.

Blessings of the Feast

No matter how you choose to celebrate your sabbats, the inclusion of food is essential. It is also just plain fun to come up with your own culinary sabbat traditions as there are no rules for this, except maybe one: share good food with family, friends, and the company of good witches.

Earth Celebration Days

While most holidays have an overtly religious theme, there is a relatively modern trend toward setting aside special days to celebrate Earth and nature. While none of the following celebrations have the commercial or widespread popularity of Christmas or Hanukkah, these environmental holidays provide an opportunity to be creative, inspire new traditions, and spread some love for Mother Earth around!

Arbour Day: The very first Arbour Day (or Arbor Day as it would be spelled in the US) was celebrated on April 10, 1872, in Nebraska City, Nebraska, USA. J. Sterling Morton, a local newspaper editor and tree-lover, instigated the event and it is estimated that more than one million trees were planted in the state of Nebraska during that first celebration. It was not declared a legal state holiday until 1885, when the date was permanently changed to April 22. The rest of the United States soon followed and then, Arbour Day spread around the world. Unlike most other holidays, Arbour Day is celebrated on different dates in different states and countries based on the best time to plant trees in that area. Celebrations include tree planting and educational opportunities to learn more about the important role that trees play on our planet.

Earth Day: April 22 is also the date that Earth Day is celebrated around the world. This holiday was born in 1970 when a junior senator from Wisconsin named Gaylord Nelson organized a national event that brought together people of all ages and walks of life to learn about the dangers and threats to the environment and take to the street in protest. The event went global in 1990 and has since grown to be known as the largest secular observance in the world.

International Day of Forests: In 2012, the United Nations General Assembly proclaimed March 21 to be the International Day of Forests to draw attention to the important role that all types of forests play in our global ecosystem. The UN encourages and promotes activities and events that raise awareness for forest conservation and tree planting.

International Dark Sky Week: The timing for this week-long celebration is very special. It is held in the month of April, during the week of the new moon, when the sky is darkest and the most stars are visible. It was founded in 2002 by an American high school student named Jennifer Barlow, and is promoted internationally by the International Dark-Sky Association and many astronomical groups and associations. The aim is to raise awareness of the damage being caused by light pollution on the environment and promote astronomy. It emphasises that a dark sky filled with stars is crucial to the health and wellbeing of all living things on the planet, and it is a heritage we are losing to light pollution.

World Soil Day: This annual event is celebrated on December 5 to honour the precious resources that soil provides for the planet. The United Nations declared the first official World Soil Day in 2014 to promote awareness of the crucial role that healthy soil plays in maintaining biodiversity and healthy ecosystems.

Personally, I like to think that every day is an earth day. My witch eyes never tire of looking out my window and seeing how nature and the environment around me shifts and changes with the turning of the Wheel of the Year. There is always something new arriving and something familiar fading away. It may not be practical to have a full-on celebration for every one of these sabbats and holidays, but it is extremely satisfying to take a moment every day to ground and centre yourself and extend your roots into the ground beneath you and your branches into the sky above and fill yourself with earth magic.

CONCLUSION

It still comes as a terrible shock to me when I meet Pagan folks who are not earth activists. We all come from different backgrounds and do not necessarily share the same life experiences or cultures, but we do all share one undeniable thing: The Earth is our home.

We all live on this beautiful, complicated, fragile, mysterious, and life-giving planet. We all depend on it being healthy and creative so that we can be that way too. A younger, edgier version of myself would laugh at what a tree-hugger I have become, but deep down inside, this feeling was always there. Reverence for the natural world and its power is hard-wired into us, and when we have our "Overview Effect" moment, we get a chance to let it out and begin to celebrate our Earth. We can then appreciate the depth and scope of how this can enrich our magic.

Earth teaches us to be creative, to make things, and to appreciate the beauty of the things around us. An overindulgence in this can cause us to become greedy and materialistic, so keeping your personal earth element in balance with the other elements is a good idea. Earth teaches us to be organized, structured, and dependable, but it also encourages us to be celebratory, decadent, and hospitable. Taking care of the mundane aspects of our lives and ensuring we have ourselves together does not mean we cannot also have a great time and enjoy ourselves.

This book was created to give you a reference and a guide to ways to connect to the element of earth in the many ways it manifests in our lives. The best way to get to know this is to actually do some of the work suggested and gift yourself the experience of how that feels. The visceral sensations of these actions will connect you.

Being an earth activist does not mean you must become a political crusader or a militant environmental warrior. It can mean that you are aware and make choices that are in the best interest of the natural world. This is the same world that you may be asking to supply you with the energy you require for your magic, so a reciprocal relationship is, at very least, fair.

Walk softly on the earth,

Dodie
TREATY ONE TERRITORY AND HOMELAND OF THE MÉTIS NATION
WINNIPEG, MANITOBA, CANADA

Appendix

EARTH CORRESPONDENCE CHART

Keywords	Grounding, sensuality, materialism, security, hospitality, career, finances, manifestation
Direction	North
Season	Winter
Time of Day	Midnight
Astrological Signs	Capricorn, Taurus, Virgo
Planets	Earth, Mercury
Tarot	Suit of Pentacles (also called Coins or Disks)
Chakra	Base (also called Muladhara or Root)
Tools	Pentacle, salt
Incense	Burgundy pitch, amber, storax, oakmoss, patchouli

Elementals	Gnomes
Colors	Green, brown, black
Gems	Emerald, jet, cat's eye, coal, kunzite, malachite
Plants	Mushrooms, moss, vines, ground-hugging food crops
Trees	Oak, cypress
Natural Objects	Stones, roots, soil
Animals	Pigs, dogs, bison, deer, badger
Deity	Gaia, Pachamama, Geb, Cernunnos, Ala, Jord, Mokosh, Prithvi
Sense	Touch
Symbol	Alchemical symbol for earth
Magical Lesson	To Keep the Silence

BIBLIOGRAPHY

Balch, James F., and Phyllis A. Balch. *Prescription for Nutritional Healing—Second Edition*. Avery Publishing Group, 1997.

Belcourt, Christi. *Medicines That Help Us—Traditional Metis Plant Use*. Gabriel Dumont Institute, 2007.

Beresford-Kroger, Diana. *Arboretum Borealis: A Lifeline of the Planet*. The University of Michigan Press 2010.

Beyerl, Paul. *The Master Book of Herbalism*. Phoenix Publishing Inc., 1984.

Culpeper, Nicholas. *Culpeper's Complete Herbal*. Arcturus Publishing Limited, 2009.

———. *Culpeper's English Physician; and Complete Herbal*. London: E. Sibly, 1794.

Cunningham, Scott. *The Complete Book of Incense, Oils and Brews*. Llewellyn Publications, 1998.

Cunningham, Scott. *Cunningham's Encyclopedia of Crystal, Gem and Metal Magic*. Llewellyn Publications, 1988.

Cunningham, Scott. *Magical Herbalism*. Llewellyn Publications, 1995.

Farrar, Janet, and Stewart Farrar. *The Witches Goddess*. Phoenix Publishing Inc., 1995.

Farrar, Janet, and Stewart Farrar. *The Witches God*. Phoenix Publishing Inc., 1989.

BIBLIOGRAPHY

Foster, Steven, and James A. Duke. *A Field Guide to Medicinal Plants and Herbs of Eastern and Central North America, 2nd. ed.* New York: Houghton Mifflin, 2000.

Foxwood, Orion. *The Candle and the Crossroads—A Book of Appalachian Conjure and Southern Root Work.* Weiser Books, 2012.

Godwin, Kerriann (Editor). *The Museum of Witchcraft: A Magical History—A Collection of Memories Celebrating 60 Years.* The Occult Art Company in conjunction with The Friends of the Boscastle Museum of Witchcraft.

Gray, Beverley. *The Boreal Herbal—Wild Food and Medicine Plants of the North.* Aroma Borealis Press, 2011.

Graves, Robert. *The White Goddess: A Historical Grammar on Poetic Myth.* Macmillan Publishers, 2013.

Hallendy, Norman. "Inuksuk (Inukshuk)." In *The Canadian Encyclopedia.* Historica Canada. Article published July 4, 2013; last edited December 8, 2020. https://www.thecanadian encyclopedia.ca/en/article/inuksuk-inukshuk.

Heselton, Philip. *A Beginner's Guide: Leylines.* Hodder and Stoughton, 1999.

Heselton, Philip. *Earth Mysteries.* Element Books Limited, 1995.

Heselton, Philip. *Magical Guardians—Exploring the Nature and Spirit of Trees.* Capall Bann Publishing, 1998.

Illes, Judika. *Encyclopedia of Spirits: The Ultimate Guide to the Magic of Fairies, Genies, Demons, Ghosts, Gods and Goddesses.* HarperCollins, 2009.

Hall, Judy. *The Crystal Bible: A Definitive Guide to Crystals.* Godsfield Press, 2003.

Lévi, Éliphas. *Transcendental Magic: Its Doctrine and Ritual*. Bracken Books, 1995.

Lima, Patrick. *The Harrowsmith Illustrated Book of Herbs*. Camden House, 1986.

Lupa. *Skin Spirits: Animal Parts in Spiritual and Magical Practice*. Stafford: Megalithica Books, 2009.

"The Megalithic Portal and Megalith Map: Megalithic Porthole Society." World-wide Ancient Site Database, Photos and Prehistoric Archaeology News with geolocation. Accessed January 2, 2021. https://www.megalithic.co.uk/index.php.

Mercier, Patricia. *The Chakra Bible: A Definitive Guide to Working with Chakras*. Godsfield Press, 2007.

Melody. *Love is in the Earth: A Kaleidoscope of Crystals*. Earth-Love Publishing House, 1991.

Native Land Digital. "Native Land." Accessed January 2, 2021. https://native-land.ca/.

Pagan Awareness Network Inc., Australia, "Sacred Ground and Acknowledgement of Country." Accessed January 2, 2021. http://www.paganawareness.net.au/wpcontent/uploads /2016/12/Brochure-acknowledgement-of-country.pdf.

Paxson, Diana. *The Essential Guide to Possession, Depossession and Divine Relationships*. Red Wheel/Weiser Books, 2015.

Robinson, Amanda. "Turtle Island." *The Canadian Encyclopedia*. Historica Canada. Article published November 06, 2018; last modified November 6, 2018. https://www.thecanadian encyclopedia.ca/en/article/turtle-island.

Tenzin-Dolma, Lisa. *Teach Yourself Astrology*. Hodder Education, 2007.

BIBLIOGRAPHY

Weed, Susun S. *Menopausal Years—The Wise Woman Way*. Ash Tree Publishing, 1992.

Winter, Sarah Kate Istra. "Working with Animal Bones: A Practical and Spiritual Guide." Sarah Kate Istra, Winter 2014.

INDEX

H